Preaching for Giving

Proclaiming Financial Stewardship with Holy Boldness

TIMOTHY J. BAGWELL

> *"Try hard to show yourself worthy of God's approval,*
> *as a laborer who needs not to be ashamed;*
> *be straightforward in your proclamation of the truth."*
> (2 Timothy 2:15, NEB)

DISCIPLESHIP RESOURCES
MATERIALS FOR GROWTH IN CHRISTIAN FAITH & LIFE
— NASHVILLE, TENNESSEE —

❖ **TO PLACE AN ORDER** OR TO INQUIRE ABOUT RESOURCES AND CUSTOMER ACCOUNTS, CONTACT:

DISCIPLESHIP RESOURCES DISTRIBUTION CENTER
P.O. BOX 6996
ALPHARETTA, GEORGIA 30239-6996

TEL: (800) 685-4370

FAX: (404) 442-5114

❖ ❖ ❖

❖ **FOR EDITORIAL INQUIRIES** AND RIGHTS AND PERMISSIONS REQUESTS, CONTACT:

DISCIPLESHIP RESOURCES EDITORIAL OFFICES
P.O. BOX 840
NASHVILLE, TENNESSEE 37202-0840

TEL: (615) 340-7068

Cover design by Ann L. Cummings.

Library of Congress Catalog Card No. 93-72190

ISBN 0-88177-127-9

DR127

Contents

To Susan,

John, and Emily

PREFACE

While working on a Doctor of Ministry degree at Garrett-Evangelical Theological Seminary, a United Methodist seminary on the campus of Northwestern University in Evanston, Illinois, I focused my study in the area of stewardship. The Ecumenical Center for Stewardship Studies (which has roots in the National Council of Churches) had negotiated with G-ETS the possibility of offering an advanced degree in this specialty area.

As a local pastor, I was particularly interested in how sermons are linked to financial stewardship. While there are many books that are compilations of stewardship sermons, very little has been written about the process of *preparing* stewardship sermons. My research at Garrett led ultimately to the birth of this book.

The world of the preacher is often filled with tension and ambiguity. I have tried to examine some of the forces that create this tension — especially in the area of preaching about stewardship — but I do not claim in my writing to have found a solution that resolves every tension. Indeed, one of the basic questions that drives the vision of this book is: "Should giving be born out of joy or duty?" My answer to that is, "Yes!" The pastor who would preach for giving — for really meaningful giving — must be prepared to walk (and to preserve) that line. The Apostle Paul understood this tension as he wrote about how grace is not law, yet it fulfills the promise of the law. How one proclaims "law" or duty makes all the difference in the world. Is it not possible to proclaim duty with joy and grace? If not, then Paul was confused.

As you read, I invite you to join me in the joy and power of this creative tension. Preachers proclaim grace, joy, and duty. All three are elements of the good news and are closely tied to preaching for giving. Any of the three proclaimed exclusively is ultimately heretical.

I am indebted to several persons who have aided in the development of this project. In particular, I would like to express my gratitude to the following:

- To Martha Bowman Memorial United Methodist Church in Macon, Georgia, for encouraging me and allowing me to have the time needed to write
- To my secretary, Carol Maynard, who is a wizard with a word processor
- To my family — Susan, John, and Emily — who patiently supported me (I plan to play baseball more often with John and Em now that I have finished.)
- To my friends who read and commented on the manuscript (Thanks for your loving honesty.)
- And to Dr. Craig Gallaway, Norma Wimberly, and the Rev. Herb Mather — all staff at the General Board of Discipleship of The United Methodist Church — who provided invaluable assistance in the preparation of the book

As you read this book, it is my hope that you will be swept up in the joyful possibilities that arise out of preaching healthy, holistic sermons related to financial stewardship. May you preach for giving with holy boldness!

Tim Bagwell
Pentecost 1993

INTRODUCTION

My parents taught me about tithing. My wife taught me
about giving. My children, John and Emily, taught me about
unmerited generosity. Their lessons created within me a new
way of looking at stewardship in my life.

I am a preacher. As a preacher, I have had times of stark
fear and dread when I thought about the upcoming fall
financial stewardship campaign. My professors in seminary
did not tell me that I was going to have to be a fundraiser.
Thrown from seminary into a small church where most of
the budget went to pay my salary, I was confronted with
the reality that if I did not provide leadership in the area
of finances, the church might have to reduce that salary.
It all seemed so crass. I thought money was a private
matter and that it was inappropriate to speak of it in public
settings.

As a preacher, I wanted to be spiritual. Money, so I
thought, was a necessary evil that had little connection to
faith and spirituality. Those wonderful laypeople at my first
church recognized my reluctance and timidity and called
my hand. "Come on, Tim," they said. "We need a financial
stewardship campaign and some good sermons on giving."

So began my journey. It is a journey that has not only
made me reconsider what it means to preach for giving,
it has completely changed my personal giving habits.

Who is the best person to preach to a local congregation
about money? If you think that it is a professional skilled
in fundraising for the church, then you are wrong. The
members of your congregation need and want to hear you,

their preacher, pastor, and friend, talk to them about faith, the Bible, God, and money.

Are you afraid? Sometimes I am, too. Preaching is an awesome responsibility, but I am convinced that you and I can make a difference from the pulpit if we learn how to preach for giving. These sermons can be joyful rather than burdensome.

As you can see, I wrote this book as a fellow struggler. In the following pages, I will explore how preachers can develop an integrated and biblically sound theology of stewardship. I will challenge preachers to acquaint themselves with their congregation by looking at church and secular history. And, finally, there will be some suggestions for developing sermons that preach — that *preach for giving*.

1 | THE PROBLEM

Preaching is hard work. It is physically and emotionally draining. The preacher reads, reflects, studies, and prays that the words uttered in worship will become the Word.

For most preachers, the preaching task is a joyful one. In spite of the rigors, preaching is anticipated rather than dreaded. In a healthy congregation, there is a normal give and take, an ebb and flow of communication between parishioners and pastor. The sermon provides an opportunity to provide pastoral care, prophecy, support, confrontation, moral guidance, and love. The preacher becomes the conduit through which the Word can provide healing and wholeness.

Great preaching is a participation in the lives of people. The preacher, rather than being separated and exalted on a pedestal, is part of the community. The sermon, be it clarion or cloudy, is given birth within the context of community as a joint effort of pastor and people. It is the reflection of living and struggling, joy and sadness, laughter and tears.

Henri Nouwen describes this kind of preacher, pastor, and person as a "wounded healer." Great preaching is cloaked in vulnerability.[1] The preacher readily acknowledges in the context of worship that he or she is a fellow struggler. Likewise, the genius of Fred Craddock's inductive preaching[2] and Don Chatfield's "Lefthanded Preaching"[3] is that these approaches invite the congregation to make a journey. The emphasis is on the commonality present in pastor and people rather than on creating a gulf between the pulpit and the pew. The preacher, for Craddock and Chatfield, becomes what Nouwen refers to as an "articulator of inner events."[4] The

1

story is told from the pulpit; the worshiper recognizes his or her connection to the story and is moved to respond. One of the most basic tasks required of the preacher is to clarify the immense confusion which arises as a person confronts the world and, after experiencing the world, confronts the inner being.

As one is able to put names on various experiences, the obstacles that can prevent the Spirit from entering are lessened. The preacher (or "articulator of inner events") is able to give these feelings and emotions linguistic titles. In so doing, she or he empowers the hearer.

A MAJOR EXCEPTION

There is, however, one aspect of preaching that is very difficult for most preachers. What is a preacher to say about money? How is the preacher to address the issue of financial stewardship and responsibility? The pragmatic realities of church life require preachers to address this issue on some level. A preacher's unwillingness to address financial issues squarely may be taken as a sign of concurrence with the view that consigns money to the role of "filthy lucre."[5]

Silence from the pulpit is powerfully eloquent in the area of financial stewardship. It is also not biblical. Statistical analysis of Jesus' message in the New Testament indicates that he raised the subjects of money and giving frequently. There are at least thirty-one statements, sermons, and teachings on the subject of money and possessions. Of the thirty-nine parables, thirteen deal directly with the question of money.[6] Jesus saw riches as a potential stumbling block as one made the inward and outward journey toward the kingdom of God.

The watchwords for most preachers, however, are timidity, lethargy, reluctance, paralysis, and embarrassment. Rarely do we confront our feelings of discomfort related to financial stewardship and ask the all-important question: "Why do I feel uncomfortable about this?"

I recall hearing a retiring preacher reflect on the change that retirement would bring to his life. In a voice tinged with sorrow, he recalled the last time he served Holy Communion to his congregation. Then, with glee, he remembered that there would be "no more stewardship campaigns and no more stewardship sermons." Everyone laughed, and I suspect there was more than one preacher who envied this retired status because of the same negative feelings about local church stewardship and preaching about money.

Could it be that the reason for this reticence about preaching on money lies in our desire to break the stereotype many people have of "church"? A Madison Avenue advertising firm surveyed unchurched people a few years ago and asked them their impressions of the church. "The problem with church," respondents said, "is that the people are always sad, or they talk about death, or they ask for money."[7] Preachers want to break this stereotype. We want church to be an exciting, lively place. Rarely do we talk about death; less often do we talk about money. Once again, however, the subconscious message may be just the opposite of what we intend — namely that we cannot talk openly about money because it is "evil" or tainted in some way. To speak or preach about money is to risk the possibility of becoming entangled in something that is "dirty."

Even for those preachers who speak or preach about money, the dialogue is many times awkward and nearly always apologetic. Scandals surrounding the finances of the electronic church — lack of accountability, misappropriation of funds, greed, manipulation of the listener, etc. — have caused many preachers to have a distaste for anything that smacks of fundraising. We do not want to be identified with "that crowd." Therefore, countless preachers have backed away.

As a consequence, the only understanding that many in our congregations have of the church and money is the perverted and twisted theology of stewardship employed by some charlatans to manipulate givers. The church needs to hear a truly biblical understanding of money and giving; but local preachers are afraid to talk about money lest they be identified with the camp of the manipulators.

What are laypeople supposed to think and believe in regard to money and Christian stewardship? Where are they to get their information related to God and their checkbook? Many follow the lead of their preacher — they simply check out with no discussion. Spirituality is not integrated with financial accountability; rather they are dichotomized. This dichotomy erodes any hope of healthy discipleship.

Stephen Hart and David Krueger recently reported in *The Christian Century* that 30 percent of mainline Protestants view work (i.e., secular life, finances) as being separate from faith. Forty-five percent see these issues as somewhat integrated. Only 25 percent acknowledge that faith and work are integral.[8] This sociological study reveals a danger for the church. If the church is unable to articulate with integrity the connection between faith and finances, there will be spiritual emptiness, and the work of God through the church will be thwarted.

Could it be that the preacher's inability to present stewardship education from the pulpit has created havoc in the church? Signs point in this direction. Many local churches are struggling to survive, and these churches feel little inclination to give money to denominational programs and missions. Denominations which formerly had no difficulty funding ministries now find themselves dealing with shrinking budgets, staff, and influence.

Out of concern for ministry and mission, the word comes from the denominational hierarchy that the local preacher needs to pay close attention to paying denominational apportionments. Motivated out of fear, guilt, and even anger, the preacher speaks to the congregation about money and spirituality. The preacher preaches on giving out of his or her emptiness. No one listens. No one responds. Few give.

THERE IS HOPE!

Before we get lost on the road to doom, however, I want to invite you to look around! There are congregations that are not following the trend. Is their success due to being located in affluent areas? There is no evidence of that. These exciting, alive, vital congregations are in blue-collar neighborhoods as well as in white-collar areas. Some are located in economically depressed areas, while others are in areas where the economy is growing.

What distinguishes these congregations? Close inspection will reveal that they have a core group of dedicated laypersons who give generously and faithfully. These laypersons call others to join them in viewing money from a spiritual perspective. The preachers in these exciting, alive churches preach joyful, challenging sermons on financial stewardship.

So there is hope. Preachers can learn how to preach unapologetic sermons about financial stewardship. These sermons do not have to be manipulative, nor do they have to browbeat the listener. Financial responsibility and accountability are very important parts of the good news. The preacher then should preach the gospel, and the gospel inevitably calls the listener to consider the integration, the interconnection among faith, spirituality, and money.

2 WHO IS LISTENING?

C ould it be that part of our problem in preaching for
giving lies in not understanding our congregations?
Some of us have moved into a parish expecting an automatic
bond to exist between us and our people. We have not invested
time or energy in getting to know our congregations. Perhaps
we know the individuals in the congregation, but that is not
the same as knowing the congregation, or the wider church
of which it is a part. What makes this church tick? What
history has molded its present? How has it evolved through
the decades and centuries? Where are its "hinge" moments
in time? What has shaped and defined the church's identity?

There are also larger issues to consider in looking at our
congregations. Our churches have been profoundly influenced
by American history. Church history in and of itself is not
enough to understand the metamorphosis of stewardship
development in America. Secular history has molded church
history; church history has influenced the evolution of
stewardship awareness and practice in the wider society.
What does it mean, for example, to preach for giving to a
congregation whose entire economic experience has been
heavily influenced by the models of free enterprise and
capitalism? Secular history and church history need to be
explored together in order to answer the question about who
is listening in our congregations.

In this chapter I want to give you a handle for understanding your congregation in this larger social and historical
context. Preaching financial stewardship sermons has a long
and unique history in America. Knowing that history will

give power and relevance to your own proclamation of the Word. To this end, we need to begin with a brief look at some of the European roots of our stewardship practices.

MARTIN LUTHER AND THE PROTESTANT REFORMATION

In many ways, the Protestant Reformation was born not simply of theological or ecclesiological issues, but of economic ones as well. Johann Tetzel was a monk whose job was to oversee the selling of indulgences in the German regions of Madgeburg and Holberstadt. The money received from these promises of divine forgiveness was used for a variety of church projects, from holy wars to the building of the new basilica of St. Peter's in Rome. The invention of the printing press enabled Tetzel to sell indulgences door to door, thus eliminating the need for confessional pilgrimages to sacred shrines. A contemporary jingle caught the decadence of this development:

> *As soon as the coin in the coffer rings, The soul from purgatory springs.* (Roland H. Bainton, *Here I Stand*)

Some members of the church asked a thirty-four-year-old doctor of theology at Wittenburg University, Martin Luther, his view on this approach to salvation. As a monk, Martin Luther had taken a vow of poverty. He had pursued salvation in the Catholic system of his day through rigorous disciplines of mind and body. As a consequence of his experience of God's overflowing grace in Christ, however, Luther began to see salvation and the value of everyday life in a new light. His response to Tetzel was nailed to the church door in Wittenburg, Germany, in the form of ninety-five Theses.[1]

In general, Luther sought to affirm the place of work, family, and material well-being in the Christian life. He condemned the perverse use of money (such as the selling of indulgences), but he believed that money and possessions were not evil in themselves. Indeed, the pursuit of material well-being through personal industry and trade was to be considered a proper Christian vocation, just as surely as praying, giving alms, and going to church.[2] As for himself, Luther later married, had a happy home life, and enjoyed the protection of the German crown against persecution by his religious opponents.

Luther's affirmation of the natural life was paralleled by other leaders of the Reformation in other parts of Europe, such as Ulrich Zwingli and John Calvin in Switzerland. Under Calvin's leadership, for example, Geneva prospered both as a center for theological education and as a magnet for new experiments in trade and business. The social and economic contexts of Protestant ideals changed on their way to America, but the basic affirmation of natural vocations and material well-being remained constant. Indeed, this affirmation has been regarded as the chief economic legacy of the Protestant Reformation.[3]

WESLEYAN ROOTS FOR STEWARDSHIP AWARENESS

The Evangelical Revival of the eighteenth century had many ramifications, not only for the British Isles but for the development of theology and ecclesiology in the New World. While this "watershed" revival was not a monopoly of John Wesley's, he certainly was the central figure around which the revival revolved. As such, the Wesleyan movement made a major contribution to the understanding and practice of stewardship both in England and in the U.S.

Wesley's own theology of stewardship is detailed in two sermons: "The Use of Money" and "The Good Steward." In the former, he reaffirmed the basic Protestant legacy in two principles — "earn all you can" and "save all you can" — but he also joined to this a third principle that added his own touch — "give all you can."[4] Wesley's spiritual formation had been influenced not only by Protestant writers (Luther and Calvin included) but also by Catholic and especially Orthodox writers from the earlier centuries of the church. As a result, his principles reflect a kind of chastening of the Protestant legacy. While affirming that Christians should be industrious and provide for their own material needs, he was not prepared to see personal wealth as an end in itself. In this way, he anticipated some of the social and economic issues that link his century with our own.

As any secular historian will tell you, the eighteenth century witnessed rapid economic change as a result of the industrial revolution. The rise of industry in England and in Europe had very mixed results. On one hand, it promised a broader distribution of wealth and signaled a potential weakening of class distinctions. Prior to the Industrial Revolution, class distinctions were simply taken for granted. Patronization of the lower classes by the nobility was the rule.[5] Now, however, a new order was emerging with the gradual development of a true middle class. This was spurred on by many factors, not the least of which was the Protestant legacy mentioned above which affirmed the value of hard work and material prosperity. The colonization of the New World was also a signal that class distinctions were becoming blurred.

At the same time, however, the Industrial Revolution also brought with it a trend toward dehumanization. Stories of sweat factories and child labor are well known. Many people moved from the country to the city in hopes of finding and making a better life. This migration caused loss of identity and poverty. Cities filled with dirty factories and sprawling slums, and workers were routinely exploited.

When Wesley observed the society of which he was a part, he became acutely aware of the disparity between the wealthy and the poor. He wrote:

I have known one in London . . . picking up from a dunghill stinking sprats [fish], and carrying them home for herself and her children. I have known another gathering bones which the dogs had left in the streets, and making broth of them to prolong a wretched life.[6]

In contrast, he also wrote about the continued wealth of the aristocracy:

Only look into the kitchens of the great, the nobility and gentry, almost without exception . . . and when you have observed the amazing waste which is made there, you will no longer wonder at scarcity, and consequently dearness, of the things which they use so much art to destroy.[7]

In one sense, the Industrial Revolution escalated the *differences* between the classes. Though economic conditions were improving in general, the rich were able to accumulate wealth far more quickly and on a much grander scale than the poor. As a result, the gap between rich and poor actually increased.

In the midst of this situation, the church was also developing a new emphasis on Christian philanthropy. The disparity between rich and poor made the need for philanthropy evident. Further, as wealth increased, more people became open and able to respond to the call for philanthropic activity. Some who settled in the New World were from debtors' prisons and were aided in their journey by wealthy nobility who had a philanthropic bent. Both inside and outside the church, humanitarian service was on the increase.

Wesley's three principles concerning the use of money were perfectly tuned to this situation. By earning and saving all they could, people were encouraged to participate in the promise of the Industrial Revolution. By giving all they could, they were exhorted to rectify its evils. For Wesley, moreover, there was an unyielding insistence on responsibility to God for the goods and gifts of creation. He was deeply concerned that the first two principles not lose their moorings to the third. Otherwise, Methodists would become "well to do" and lose their religious zeal and fervor. The taste for "luxury" could become an attitude on the part of the common person to get whatever was available at the expense of others.

Particularly in the latter part of his life, Wesley became blunt in his condemnation of accumulated wealth. This arose out of a cynicism related to the Methodist movement, now almost a million strong. Wesley felt that Methodists no longer had the fervor to move toward perfection. He believed that this lack of focus on spiritual issues was motivated primarily by the love of money. He stated that not one Methodist in one hundred was able to overcome this sin. In what he thought might be his final sermon, he rebuked his followers for their disobedience to the Lord in this area. The increase in wealth brought about a decrease in godliness, according to Wesley. While he wanted Methodists to care for their own and their family's needs, he "regarded surplus accumulation as sinful in itself or as at the least an irresistible temptation to sin."[8] Thus, he set high standards for himself and others to follow.

Some have questioned how deeply or fully Wesley understood the distance between the economic conditions of society and the spiritual disciplines of the individual. Wesley's primary focus for change seems to have been on the piety and sanctification of the individual. He taught the worth of the human soul. As a result, in some ways, the very tenets upon which the Methodist movement was based may have played into the hands of an unrestrained industrial economy. The worth of the human soul could become perverted to mean that every person must fend for himself or herself (survival of the fittest). Calvinists could rationalize the continued existence of a gap between rich and poor by pointing to God's preordained place for every individual.

Even the Methodist insistence on individual response to grace, however, could be turned to the purposes of industrialists who wanted to manipulate the honesty and thrift of the masses. Thus, while some have praised the Wesleyan revival for helping to avert a bloody revolution such as the French experienced, others have blamed the movement for cutting short those historical forces that might otherwise have changed the class system in England more radically.

For his own part, Wesley grew up in poverty. His father, Samuel, was the priest in one of England's lowest paying parishes. With a wife and nine children to support, family responsibilities were great. Samuel once even served a term in debtors' prison. John's election as a fellow at Lincoln College, however, changed his financial position. While Wesley and his father shared the same vocation, they were on completely different financial levels. Charles White has written of how the new situation presented unforeseen challenges to Wesley's conscience:

> One incident that happened to him at Oxford changed his perspective on money. He had just finished buying some pictures for his room when one of the chambermaids came to his door. It was a winter day and he noticed that she had only a thin linen gown to wear for protection against the cold. He reached into his pocket to give her some money for a coat, and he found he had little left. It struck him that the Lord was not pleased with how he had spent his money. He asked himself: "Will Thy Master say, 'Well done, good and faithful steward?' Thou hast adorned thy walls with the money that might have screened this poor creature from the cold! O justice! O mercy! Are not the pictures the blood of this poor maid?"[9]

This incident changed the way he lived. Ever the meticulous keeper of a journal, Wesley wrote an accounting of his financial expenses. In one year he made thirty pounds, lived on twenty-eight, and gave away two. The next year his income doubled but he lived on twenty-eight pounds and gave away thirty-two. The third year he gave away sixty-two pounds while living on the same amount as in the previous two years. One year his income was over 1,400 pounds. He gave away all except thirty pounds.[10] During his lifetime Wesley gave away more than 30,000 pounds. At his death he was a pauper, having less than ten pounds in his possession.

Out of compassion, Wesley threw his lot in with the working class. He was enormously popular with them and routinely preached to massive audiences. There is a paradox here because, in terms of financial *income*, John Wesley was not one of them. With the enormous sums he made from preaching and writing, he could readily have lived as one of England's wealthiest individuals. Further, according to White, thirty pounds was sufficient in Wesley's day to support a comfortable way of life.[11] Thus, as Francis McConnell has written: "It is doubtful . . . if Wesley fully appreciated the bleakness of the age. . . . Wesley was a vital person, running over with life. . . . Like others, he did not think much about some of the hardships."[12] Nevertheless, in choosing to give away the vast majority of his income, Wesley showed himself ready to practice *all* of the advice that he preached to others — earn all you can, save all you can, give all you can.

For our purposes, then, in relation to the historical development of stewardship, we can summarize Wesley's legacy in terms of three basic ideas (parallel with, but not to be confused with, the three principles of his sermon "On the Use of Money").

1. *All wealth for the Christian comes from God.* He recognized that all we have comes from God; it is entrusted to us for a time, and we are not to use these gifts indiscriminately, but "as the Lord pleases."[13] According to Wesley we have received much, including soul, heart, mind, all

the members of our body, speech, worldly goods (including money), health, pleasing personality, knowledge, influence, time, and grace. He asserted that humans are stewards of these gifts only for this life; when our spirit returns to God, our stewardship ends.[14]

2. *There will be a time to account for our stewardship.* Wesley set forth a minutely detailed inventory of questions he felt we could anticipate at the time of judgment. In his sermon, "The Good Steward," he listed at least sixty-one questions having to do with how we use our soul, body, will, and worldly goods. His questions, in typical Wesley fashion, were blunt and piercing.

3. *Christians are given money so that they can give it away.* In "On the Danger of Increasing Riches," Wesley wrote, "Do not you know that God entrusted you with that money (all above what buys necessaries for your families) to feed the hungry, to clothe the naked, to help the stranger, the widow, the fatherless; and indeed, as far as it will go, to relieve the wants of all mankind? How can you, how dare you, defraud your Lord, by applying it to any other purpose?"[15]

We might say that Wesley brought forward the Protestant emphasis on industry and material well-being, but he also brought this back into greater tension with some of the earlier teachings of the church that stressed the virtues of a simple life. He did not advocate a return to Monasticism, but neither was he ready to baptize the accumulation of wealth per se. His theology of stewardship was practical in nature and relational in concept. His emphasis on "holy living," though focused largely on the individual, had a profound impact on Britain and on those who left Britain to come to the New World. We shall look again at Wesley's legacy when we discuss the American scene in more detail below. For

now, however, we need to look at one more major Protestant
stream that has contributed significantly to the historical
development we are tracing.

THE PURITANS AND STEWARDSHIP

One of the primary groups to be born out of the
Protestant Reformation was the Puritans. These English
followers of Calvin became highly important not only in the
ecclesiastical history of America, but also in secular history.
Out of this movement came the Protestant work ethic which
played a major role in shaping U.S. capitalism. Max Weber's
watershed book of the early 1900s, *The Protestant Ethic and
the Spirit of Capitalism*, attempted to show that the development of Protestantism in the U.S. went hand in hand with the
development of capitalism. Puritan influences can be seen
within almost all denominational expressions of Protestant
thought in America.

The Puritan settlers came to America with a strong sense
of "calling." The cause that led them to make the dangerous
Atlantic voyage was righteous in their eyes. God had chosen
them and set them apart. They believed that the promise of
the New World went hand in hand with the promise of God.
Money, possessions, fortune, all of these were gifts of God.
William Perkins (1558-1602) wrote, "If we happen to have
inherited much property we are to enjoy it in good conscience
as a blessing and gift of God."[16] Colonial America took such
statements to heart. Their cause was a holy one. The land
had been given to them as a gift. They were determined to be
true to their "calling." (Unfortunately, little sensitivity was
shown to natives from whom the land was taken.)

Highly visible individuals such as Benjamin Franklin
embraced and celebrated the wisdom of this evolving work
ethic of Protestantism. In *Poor Richard's Almanac* and in his
autobiography, he shares quotes from the Bible, such as:

"Seest thou a man diligent in his business? He shall stand before kings" (Proverbs 22:29). While Franklin was a deist, his values were strongly influenced by a strict Calvinistic father.[17]

As we saw in the case of Luther, the Catholic Church's emphasis on the virtue of poverty was reversed within the context of Puritanism. Colonial America was generally much more attuned to the rights and freedoms of individuals than to anything that smacked of pronouncements or edicts from the church. The emphasis on freedom certainly focused on issues of experiential faith and religion, but it also extended to specific affirmations of the right of the individual to accumulate and dispose of material property.

Furthermore, while it would be inaccurate to depict the Puritans as a purely materialistic people, it is true that their single-minded approach to life enabled many to accumulate significant wealth. Wasting time by enjoying recreation or amusement was viewed as sinful. Industrious Christians thus focused on their work as a "calling" (compare Luther's concept of Christian vocation). Likewise, eighteenth century Methodists (also influenced by Puritanism) were known for their "methodical" approach to life and for their willingness and eagerness to put in a full day of hard work to earn a just wage.[18] Thus, even accumulating wealth was not their sole objective, many Puritans (and those influenced by Puritan culture) became quite successful as a result of the work ethic.

True to their Protestant heritage, the Puritans believed that God was involved in all aspects of life. Those who accumulated wealth could, therefore, explain such prosperity as a sign of their faithfulness to God's calling. If opportunity for profit presented itself to the individual, the conscientious Christian took advantage of the situation. Refusing to do so would indicate an unwillingness to be a good steward and would reflect a desire to turn one's back on God's presence and call.

At the same time, some influential Puritans recognized the danger of unbridled materialism and rang a note of caution. Cotton Mather (1663-1727) coined the famous phrase: "Religion begot prosperity and the daughter devoured the mother."[19] Likewise, William Perkins provided a summary caution for Puritans in the use of money (compare Wesley):

> We must so use and possess the goods we have, that the use and possession of them may tend to God's glory, and the salvation of our souls. . . . Our riches must be employed to necessary uses. These are: First, the maintenance of our own good estate and condition. Secondly, the good of others, specially those that are of our family or kindred. . . . Thirdly, the relief of the poor. . . . Fourthly, the maintenance of the church of God, and true religion. . . . Fifth, the maintenance of the Commonwealth.[20]

THE EVOLUTION OF FINANCIAL STEWARDSHIP IN AMERICA

Luther, Calvin, Wesley, the Puritans — each of these made specific contributions to the conceptions and practices of Christian stewardship that European settlers brought with them to Colonial America. Taken together, the elements of this legacy contained a number of real tensions and ambiguities — such as that between the affirmation of prosperity and the appeal to give sacrificially. The uniqueness of the American situation, moreover, turned this legacy in new directions and heightened the tensions in specific ways.

The primary factor that affected the practice of stewardship in the New World was the American experiment with the separation of church and state. In the European or Old World context, the state largely controlled the finances of the church — either through the patronage of local landholding princes, such as in Luther's Germany, or through the imposition of taxes, such as the parish "tithe" in the Church of England. To be sure, there were instances of voluntary giving — such as the pooling of resources among Methodists to build a preaching house in London, but the finances of the *official* church continued to be controlled by the state.

The situation in the New World, by contrast, was based on the principle of separation of church and state. Indeed, this was a primary objective of the Puritans who left England to settle in America. Separating church finances from state control, however, brought both freedom and responsibility. On the one hand, the state would no longer be allowed to exercise control over the church. On the other, the church would ever after be dependent on voluntary contributions to support its various activities and ministries. As a result, churches in America found themselves having to talk about the old themes of giving in new ways.

For one thing, churches in the young country had to deal in new ways with the issue of ministerial support. In Wesley's England, the minister's support came out of the parish tithe. In America, such a system was suspect. The Reverend John Cotton, an outstanding Congregational leader, stated clearly that magistrates should not be involved in the securing of ministerial support. He advocated that the minister's support come from voluntary contributions rather than from taxation which he said had always been accompanied by pride, contention, and sloth.[21]

The shift toward voluntary contributions thus promised a new level of personal accountability and integrity among pastors and parishioners. In practical terms, this meant a new way of receiving offerings, such as that practiced in the Congregational Church in New England by the middle of the seventeenth century. In Volume Two of the *Massachusetts Historical Collection*, we find a description of how the Boston

Congregational Church received its offering. Following the afternoon service, and prior to the dismissal of the assembly, one of the deacons would say: "Brethren of the congregation, as God has prospered you, so offer freely." Hierarchy was important, so persons of distinction responded first, followed by the elders. Then each man (not woman) would go forward with his offering, taking it to where a deacon was seated and deposit it in a box provided for that purpose.

The importance of voluntary giving in the New World was also heightened by the development of missions. Immediately following the Revolutionary War, most Protestant denominations had only a vision of self-preservation and maintenance. With the close of the eighteenth century and the beginning of the nineteenth century, however, the concept of missions came to new prominence. The Baptists were motivated by William Carey to begin an emphasis on missions which moved the church beyond the status quo. Thus, ministerial support was not the only ministry that needed to be met through voluntary contributions. Carey believed that all of life was bound up in stewardship, and his sole purpose in life was to share Christ with persons living in India.

Such a movement naturally required the accumulation of resources beyond church maintenance. The missionary movement began in England and quickly spread to Colonial America. By the 1790s the Presbyterian, Dutch Reformed, Baptist, and Congregational Churches all had missionary outreach programs in place.[22] While some of the initial American interest in missions was concentrated on other lands, the primary focus was on new settlements as the nation moved west. Much of the Methodist focus was on establishing Sunday schools. Efforts were made to place a Sunday school in every community not having one. Rather substantial sums were collected for this missionary outreach program, and full-time persons were employed to carry out the goal.

The new situation of voluntary giving *promised* much, but it also *expected* much. Since "giving" was no longer enforced by the state, people were free in a new way both to give and to withhold giving. Methodist congregations in the New World could depend on a well-organized system of ministerial supply,[23] but they were not always dependable in financially supporting their preachers. Bishop Francis Asbury allegedly favored keeping salaries low, lest prosperity should encourage the traveling preachers to marry and locate (cf. Wesley). Some Methodist congregations seemed all too eager to quote Asbury on this point in order to rationalize their meager support. Without adequate motivation, the virtues of voluntary giving could sink toward the vices of arbitrary giving.

In sum, we may say that three factors created a new situation for the church in America — the separation of church and state, the rise of voluntary giving, and the growing emphasis on missionary outreach. Voluntary contributions were a must, since the state provided no support for the churches. In this context, the ability to motivate laypersons to give became an issue for the church and leaders in a way that it had never been before.

SETTING THE STAGE FOR STEWARDSHIP PREACHING

From the beginning, preaching in America has been consumer-oriented. Separation of church and state created a situation in which people were free as never before to view the church and its services as a commodity — to give or not to give, depending on whether they felt that a particular congregation was doing what it should be doing. In this setting, preachers had to raise their own support, as well as motivate parishioners to give to other causes. The sermon itself became one of the primary vehicles for such motivation, and no one better epitomizes the character of early American preaching than George Whitefield.

Whitefield was viewed by many as the most powerful pre-Revolutionary preacher in America. Heavily influenced by Wesley, Whitefield made several trips to America and helped create the uniquely American preaching style. After founding and establishing Bethesda Orphanage for Boys in Savannah, Georgia, Whitefield moved up the Eastern coast to raise money for the orphanage. Ben Franklin, one of Whitefield's admirers, attended some of the preaching services in Philadelphia. In his *Autobiography*, Franklin humorously teased his friend, Whitefield, about how the latter used his sermons to raise money for the orphanage:

> Mr. Whitefield . . . preached up this charity, and made large collections, for his eloquence had a wonderful power over the hearts and purses of his hearers, of which I myself was an instance. I did not disapprove of the design, but as Georgia was then destitute of materials and workmen, and it was proposed to send them from Philadelphia at a great expense, I thought it would have been better to have built the house here, and brought the children to it. This I advised; but he was resolute in his first project, rejected my counsel, and I therefore refused to contribute. I happened, soon after, to attend one of his sermons, in the course of which I perceived he intended to finish with a collection, and I silently resolved he should get nothing from me. I had in my pocket a handful of copper money, three or four silver dollars, and five pistoles in gold. As he proceeded I began to soften, and concluded to give the coppers. Another stroke of his oratory made me ashamed of that, and determined me to give the silver; and he finished so admirably that I emptied my pocket wholly into the collector's dish, gold and all. At this sermon there was also one of our club, who, being of my sentiments

respecting the building in Georgia, and suspecting a collection might be intended, had by precaution emptied his pockets before he came from home. Towards the conclusion of the discourse, however, he felt a strong desire to give, and applied to a neighbour who stood near him, to borrow some money for the purpose. The application was unfortunately made, to perhaps the only man in the company who had the firmness not to be affected by the preacher. His answer was, "At any other time, Friend Hopkinson, I would lend to thee freely; but not now, for thou seems to be out of thy right senses."[24]

Such was the power of Whitefield's persuasive ability. Such was the nature of preaching to a voluntary audience in America. George Whitefield's influence, particularly in the Middle Colonies, extended beyond the British churches to the Dutch and the German. Sydney Ahlstrom tells of a German woman who, after hearing Whitefield preach, asserted that she in all her life had never been so edified, though she understood not a word of English.[25]

Whitefield is said to have preached powerfully in Boston. When he left the city to travel to Northampton for a visit with Jonathan Edwards, 30,000 Bostonians gathered on the Common to bid him farewell. Whitefield's preaching had the dual thrust of stewardship (providing money for his orphanage) and evangelism. Of preachers he had a dim view: "I am verily persuaded, the Generality of Preachers talk of an unknown, unfelt Christ. And the reason why congregations have been so dead, is because dead men preach to them."[26]

Such pre-Revolutionary preaching brought about a great and general awakening among clergy and laity. This set the stage for further evangelistic revivals to come and certainly brought together the concepts of informal worship, preaching, stewardship, and evangelism. The main thrust of American Protestantism still combines these emphases.

Wesley's theological heritage influenced Whitefield and, in some ways, supported the new role of the preacher and the sermon in relation to giving. The Wesleyan emphasis on holiness and sanctification moved the focus of faithfulness from attention to worship to a concern with living out the faith. Wesley's influence helped Whitefield stay focused on the need for individual response. The faithful felt God's power in their lives and were then called to personalize this power through holy living. It was not enough for the individual to simply experience God's presence. Holiness and sanctification in Whitefield's preaching brought a sense of accountability to those who responded. Religious experience and expression were not separated from one's everyday life. Rather, an awareness of the world and its needs was a vital part of the preaching event and the personal response.

Whitefield's approach to preaching for giving was followed by many other preachers in America, including Jonathan Edwards in New England. The developing style had certain characteristics. In essence, the liturgical order of worship became secondary to expediency and spontaneity in preaching. What counted was not the maintenance of a traditional order in worship, but the achievement of significant evangelistic and monetary results in response to the sermon. This style set the stage for evangelical revivals and the zeal for mission that followed in America.

This new flexibility in worship and preaching was, of course, fraught with danger. While the revivalistic approach to preaching allowed for possibilities such as connected series of sermons and special attention to current events, there was always the danger of the abuse of scripture. At times, the Bible was really quite secondary in the sermon and service of worship. The text was only a short word of scripture just before the sermon. After a specific subject was determined, a text was found that would address the already-chosen theme. While the sermon ceased to be properly exegetical, it was more and more inclined to exalt the prophetic role of the preacher.[27] This gave the preacher the opportunity to focus on a constricted choice of subjects based on personal desire. Under such circumstances, the Bible was relegated to the status of a secondary resource.

Over time, the development of revivalistic preaching caused the church in some segments to lose the invaluable corrective of scripture against privatization. The individual, both clergy and lay, became increasingly important. Personal experience took precedence over church tradition and history. The scope of this evolution eventually affected not only patterns of worship and sermon, but also church architecture. The centrality of the altar table in Europe, for example, gave way to the centrality of the pulpit. The preached word (and consequently the preacher) took precedence over the liturgy. The largest bodies of Protestantism (Methodist, Baptist, Presbyterian), along with dozens of smaller denominations, were susceptible to the architectural evolution that reflected a change in the view of liturgy and the role of preaching.

THE HISTORICAL DEVELOPMENT OF STEWARDSHIP SERMONS

All of the factors we have so far discussed set the stage in America for sermons focused specifically — one might say almost self-consciously — on the subject of *stewardship*. To be sure, sermons on giving had been preached before (cf. Wesley's "The Good Steward"); but it was not until the early nineteenth century in America that one would witness the full-fledged formal product of the historical metamorphosis that we have been tracing.

Salstrand writes that one of the earliest sermons to treat stewardship as a formal subject was that of the Reverend Leonard Bacon, pastor of First Congregational Church in New Haven, Connecticut.[28] In 1832 he delivered a sermon entitled "The Christian Doctrine of Stewardship." His primary question was: "What is the right use of property on Christian principles?" The sermon reveals his answer: Scripture obliges people to regard all property as a gift from God. The individual is charged with managing a trust that has temporarily been placed into his or her hands. A day of reckoning and judgment will come. The work of the Lord has exclusive priority. These themes are similar, of course, to what we saw earlier in the preaching of Wesley and others. What has changed is the level at which the subject now becomes formalized in the preacher's repertoire.

The formalization of the concept of stewardship on the American scene is further demonstrated in the work of several preachers. For example, the Reverend Pharcellus Church, pastor of First Baptist Church, Rochester, New York, wrote a book entitled *The Philosophy of Benevolence*. Salstrand lists several chapters that reveal the contents of the book: "Vindication of Systematic Benevolence," "Alarming Consequences of Having a Passion for Wealth Predominate," "The Proportion of our Income Which we are Bound to Devote to God," and "Doctrine of Entire Consecration."

Likewise, Charles Finney was an ardent proponent of stewardship as a focal point for faith and preaching. Like Wesley and other European antecedents, Finney felt that everything is a gift of God and that humans are simply trustees. Like Bacon and other American counterparts, Finney's very definition of conversion drew the concept of stewardship closer and closer to the center. Thus, a convert is one who has submitted everything to God and has made a free surrender of all things for God's use and pleasure.

> In his *Lectures of Professing Christians*, delivered in New York City, he set forth seven accountabilities of God's stewards, namely: use of time, talents, the influence exerted on one's contacts, manner of using possessions,

one's soul, the souls of others, and the sentiments maintained and propagated.[29]

What we see here is an agenda for stewardship preaching that developed in greater and greater detail as a response to the peculiar problems and possibilities of capitalistic economy in America. The realities of market economy, private property, and increased wealth are everywhere assumed, as is the separation of church and state, the need for ministerial support, and the appeal for world missions. All of this, moreover, affected the theological content of American sermons in specific ways.

Consider, for example, the theological concept that everything we are and have comes from God — we are simply "trustees" of God's gifts. This was one of the most widely used theological concepts in the stewardship preaching of the nineteenth century. This "trustee" concept was sometimes linked (in the manner of the Puritans) with fear of judgment as the motivation for generosity. Jonathan Edwards in particular used such imagery in his famous sermon, "Sinners in the Hands of an Angry God." Above all, such imagery challenged the capitalistic notion of the "self-made" individual. To be a good trustee or steward in this sense was not to boast of self-sufficiency but to practice gratitude and generosity, and thus to avoid negative judgment at the time of death.

Another theological conception was promoted by Lyman Abbott, Henry Ward Beecher's successor in Brooklyn. Abbott believed that the objective of all business — as well as every other activity — should be the "promotion of the kingdom of God." Notice the use of the word *promotion* by Abbott. Prior to Abbott, this word had been used frequently in business circles but only rarely within the context of the church. Abbott thus borrowed a traditional business word and turned it toward more sanctified purposes. Abbott was convinced that if one would focus on promoting the kingdom of God, then she or he could be assured of God's help — both in one's personal finances and as "a means for the service of God and the enrichment of humanity."[30] In this way, Abbott tried to blend the Puritan conception that God blesses the faithful giver with what he saw as the motivational power of capitalism at its best.

A third theological motivator of this period focused neither on divine judgment nor on financial success per se, but struck a kind of compromise between the two in order to "win the world for Christ." On the one hand, to reach the whole world for Christ clearly required substantial financial backing. Thus, broad acceptance was given to the idea that God calls certain persons to make a great deal of money. Some persons have money-making talent. To bury such talent would be just as wrong as burying a talent for preaching. On the other hand, the ability to make money in the capitalist system was not an end in itself. Rather, people from all occupations should be as concerned and involved in world missions as are missionaries themselves. Thus, Josiah Strong, pastor of the Central Congregational Church of Cincinnati, declared that the sole business of Christians in this world is the expansion of Christ's kingdom.[31] In this way, the old tension between prosperity and sacrificial giving received a specifically American and capitalist spin.

The trend toward more and more formalized doctrines of stewardship continued throughout the century, but the first official denominational statement was not formulated until 1858 by the Presbyterians. The General Assembly received a report from the "Systematic Benevolence Committee" concerning the doctrine and duty of Christian stewardship. Salstrand is helpful in condensing the statement:

> Every man is a steward of God in the use and management of the talents, time, and substance which God has entrusted to him," the statement commenced. The trust

must be fulfilled "for God's glory and the good of the world," it continued. Contributions of material wealth for religious purposes with Scriptural motives and manner was set forth as Christian duty and "a part of true piety" as fully as any other spiritual activity. The statement warned that Christians were not at liberty to "neglect or slightly perform at his own pleasure" the ministry of giving. Even more convicting was the committee's judgment that a person could not be a "consistent Christian" and fail to be a "man of beneficence" as well as a man of prayer. Pray and pay go together in the establishment and maintenance of Christ's kingdom. Offering of property to God was summarized as a vital part of early church worship. . . . In conclusion the report stated that the "grace of charity" could be strengthened by exercise.[32]

Statements such as this helped preachers to formulate theological themes for their sermons. Formal statements also placed the polity of the church clearly behind the preachers, as each one sought to motivate parishioners to give. All of this reflected, moreover, the evolution of traditional Protestant conceptions of money and giving on the peculiarly voluntaristic and individualistic soil of the American church.

REDISCOVERING OUR VOICE

When we ask in America today, "Who is listening to stewardship sermons?", we need to keep this history in mind. Of course the church has not stood still since the nineteenth century, nor has society; but the basic dynamics that we have traced remain very much alive in the American consciousness. Indeed, the inherited tensions between prosperity and simplicity, individual freedom and communal vision have actually intensified with the separation of church and state and the spread of market economy. Americans today are more affluent than ever. They give more than ever. Yet they also live in an environment where the motivations for giving are often confused and where the role of the church is increasingly marginal. This situation contains both peril and promise for those who are called to preach for giving.

The chief peril is that the dynamics of individualism, market economy, and separation of church and state will drive the church further and further away from its proper role in the formation of communal vision and mission. A parishioner of mine once remonstrated that he needn't give to the church since his tax dollars already supported the "down and out" persons in America. His logic was that our social welfare system, paid for by taxes, fulfills Jesus' call to help the "least of these" (Matthew 25:31-46).

In some ways it's hard to argue with that logic. Historically, it is accurate. The ethical concern of our social welfare system — whatever we may think of its financial methods — owes a great deal to the moral vision of the church. Where, after all, did the state receive its mandate to care for the poor if not from the biblical roots of the Judaeo-Christian heritage? At the same time, however, we cannot simply live on the spiritual capital of the past. There is every evidence in America today that the moral fabric of society is breaking down. One remarkable recent study suggests that the principle of individual freedom in our country is increasingly isolated and fragmented from those biblical roots which historically helped to shape and refine our vision of community.[33]

The situation is not helped any by the practices of charlatan preachers who abuse biblical images in order to gather wealth for their own empires. In a society ruled in many ways by market dynamics and individualistic promotions, we shall certainly continue to see seedy examples of sermonic manipulation; but we cannot afford to let that block our vision of vital congregations where genuine stewardship really does make a difference in communities and in the world. Pastors and other leaders simply cannot afford to sidestep stewardship issues for fear that they will be linked with the wild-eyed hucksters of the marketplace. Our people need real, true, life-giving motives for giving and living in the joy of God.

Therefore, despite the perils, the role of the church in America today is also full of promise — if only we can rediscover our voice. We need to remember and affirm that many of today's finest colleges, universities, hospitals, homes for orphans and widows, retirement centers, and ministries for the poor had their origin in the missional outreach of the church. We need to recapture the kind of *communal vision* for stewardship that made such outreach possible in the first place. And we need to ask what is happening to many of these same institutions as their vision is severed more and more from the church in all but the most formal ways. Above all, we need to help our people regain a vision of their proper and joyful role in the moral and spiritual fabric of society.

As the church regains such a vision, it will also rediscover fresh life and joy in itself. Giving will become connected again to significant missional programs rather than focusing on nebulous maintenance appeals, or on manipulative personal campaigns of dubious integrity. In short, the church will come much closer to the New Testament definition of "church." It is no accident that membership, attendance, and giving in most mainline denominations have plummeted as they have abdicated their proper stewardship roles either to the state or to the manipulations of the electronic church. As the mainstream church rediscovers its missional vision and voice, it can move once again from irrelevance to leadership, and it can do this without sinking to the level of media manipulation or privatized religion.

An increased awareness of genuine need and a proactive response to that need will give the church new life and focus. Numerous churches and denominations are rediscovering that laity give when there is a specific, designated need. This, after all, is part of our heritage. We are a people who have always heard and known that our wealth is not an end in itself. What we need are preachers, leaders, and sermons that reconnect us with the *best* in our own traditions of faith and stewardship practice. We need to rediscover our voice.

Being aware of our history and letting it inform our present-day reality helps us to know our people better. It also provides context and insight for our preaching. United Methodist Bishop Richard Looney warns us, however, not to become slaves to nostalgia.[34] While we can learn from yester-year, we must not make the mistake of thinking that answers to our financial stewardship problems lie solely in the past. God's Spirit is dynamically future-oriented! We use the past, not to protect the status quo, but to push off into the future. Knowing and understanding congregational history, denomi-national history, as well as secular history reminds us of where we are standing now as we move forward into deeper reflection on the communal and relational vision of the Bible — the true bedrock of preaching for giving.

3 BIBLICALLY SOUND THEOLOGY

One of the primary reasons many of us fear preaching on stewardship is because we know that we will be preaching out of our emptiness. Seminary training may have helped us develop an understanding of systematic theology, but for many of us, that training never really permeated the practical and motivational issues of stewardship. Our "head" theology has never become our "heart" theology. Indeed, we may even have excused ourselves from theological discussions concerning stewardship for fear of being tagged as one of those who manipulate the heart.

It is my contention that our people are starving for biblically sound reasons for giving. A layperson made an exceptionally large gift to a television evangelist. His local pastor heard of the gift and went to visit the man. The pastor questioned the man's gift, "Why did you make the gift to that ministry when your local church needed the money?" The layperson's reply was shockingly simple: "You never asked and you never gave me a reason to give." How do we share with our people a reason for generous giving? We need a cogent, coherent, biblically sound theology that spans the distance between our head and our heart.

United Methodist Bishop Ken Carder has offered a remarkable outline for practical theology based on three questions: "Who is God? What is God doing? What does that have to do with me?"[1] The Bishop's words also define the task of preaching for giving. We must challenge our congregations to face these questions.

1. **"Who is God?"** The first question is theological in the strict sense. In the midst of all the things that crowd our busy lives, what does it really mean to know, love, proclaim, and worship the living God? Loving and praising God are profoundly connected with the development of healthy stewardship. Indeed, the biblical picture of God's love and faithfulness is our main source of a generous communal vision.

2. **"What is God doing?"** The second question is a historical question, spanning biblical and church history to the present. When we ask this question, we are in a healthy dialogue concerning the historical reality of God in the world and in our lives. Gaining insight into what God has done and is doing in our world is sure to release the springs of healthy stewardship.

3. **"What does that have to do with me?"** Here is the question that invites commitment. In distinction from strictly biblical, theological, and historical questions, this one is ethical; but it is not academic. One cannot encounter the Word or be involved in sound theology without moving to the question of commitment. Inevitably the intangible must become tangible. Biblical and theological reflection — indeed, dialogue with God in sermon, prayer, and worship — points ultimately to this final stewardship question.

Bishop Carder's questions provide a sure foundation for the preacher who would develop a biblically sound theology of stewardship. The preacher's task, then, is to engage the congregation in such a way that these questions are commonly and frequently asked. This chapter will respond primarily to the first two questions posed by Bishop Carder. The remainder of the book will reflect on the third.

LANGUAGE FOR GOD?

Christians have traditionally spoken of God in terms of the Trinity. The trinitarian model holds many mysteries, but it also opens a specifically Christian window for understanding who God is. Trinitarian theology reflects a yearning, tenacious, and compassionate God. In comparison with some forms of strict religious monotheism, trinitarian language portrays God as interacting with the world. God even suffers with and for the world. According to trinitarian thought, God is not like a great or distant individual, existing in splendid isolation. Rather, God is love — the love revealed in Father, Son, and Holy Spirit.

The church has always recognized that language for God has limits. Finite language can never completely comprehend the being and character of the infinite God. Thus, when we address God as Father, Son, and Spirit, we do not imply that God is male rather than female. Gender is not the meaning of these terms in the Bible. The biblical language does, however, convey an extremely important insight that the church has been at pains to preserve throughout the centuries: God is *personal* and *relates* to human beings in *personal* ways.

When Jesus taught his followers to address God as *Abba* ("Father" or "Daddy" in Aramaic), he was preserving this sense of intimate personal relationship. His "naming" of God in this way reflected an important debate with the orthodox Judaism of his day. First-century Jewish religious leaders often portrayed God as "other, apart, removed." The Old Testament references to God's mercy and loving-kindness had in many ways become overlain with rules and restrictions that served to separate people from God, making God appear distant, foreboding, and hard to approach. When Jesus referred to God in familiar and endearing terms, he risked being charged with blasphemy. His purpose was to nurture *personal relationship* and to invite *communal vision*, not to promote paternalistic power.

Our use of trinitarian language in this chapter follows that of Jesus. It is a means of focusing on the importance of personal relationship with God. It is a sign of God's involvement, optimism, and solidarity with us in all things. God never gives up. The Bible is a hopeful document! Woven through its pages are the stories of men and women who have succeeded and failed. Even in the failure, however, there is hope! Trinitarian language is a true reflection of the unaltering reality of God's love, and this love is foundational for a theology of genuine stewardship tuned to the needs of the church today.

GOD OF CREATION AND COVENANT

God has always desired a *relationship* with human beings. In the creation story, God is portrayed as the source of life, but this does not place God at a distance from creation. The creation story of Genesis 1 describes a dialogue with God that gives Adam and Eve a relationship to God and to each other, as well as a relationship to the world. Likewise, the creation story of Genesis 2 breathes relationship. Adam is invited to share in God's creative activity as he names the living creatures (Genesis 2:18-20). At the point of failing in their responsibilities, Adam and Eve are still in relationship with God. God looks for them in the garden, and in a wonderful, loving, and maternal metaphor, the writer pictures God making garments for Adam and Eve as they leave the Garden of Eden (Genesis 3:21).

Thus, in Genesis, God longs for relationship in spite of human failure. Indeed, God comes again to Cain and Abel, and to all those ancestors — male and female — who come after them in the long account of the beginnings of civilization. Throughout the story, there is a powerful tone of interdependence. God does not coerce relationship. God persuades, invites, and woos human beings to receive the relationship for which they are created.

Abraham and Sarah also responded to this creating, personal, and relating God. Raised in a pagan culture, Abraham and Sarah had every reason to think of God as a deity to be feared. The gods of Abraham's day had to be appeased in order to win their favor. Certainly they were not considered "friends." According to scripture, however, Abraham and his family came to understand God in a different way. Having pitched their camp under the oaks of Mamre, a rugged hill country about fifteen miles south of what is today Jerusalem, Abraham sat in the tent opening and talked with God. God was his friend. They called God *El Shaddai*, freely translated as "The Almighty God." From their own experience of God's love, care, guidance, and faithfulness, they concluded that this Almighty God was also the creator of the sun, moon, stars, and earth. God was in relationship with Abraham and the family as an unseen member of the group.

A covenant, or agreement, grew out of this relationship between Abraham and "El Shaddai." "Look toward heaven and count the stars, if you are able to count them. . . . So shall your descendants be. . . . I will establish my covenant between me and you, and your offspring after you throughout their generations, for an everlasting covenant, to be God to you and to your offspring after you" (Genesis 15:5, 17:7). Indeed, God also promised that all the nations of the earth would be blessed as a result of the blessing to Abraham and his family (Genesis 26:4). What a promise! What a legacy!

The covenant relationship that God offered was not, however, automatic, passive, or one-sided. The relationship held the promise of shalom, peace, wholeness, well-being, and community; but it was made complete in the faithful response of the people. A faithful life is the mirror image in human experience of God's covenant promise and faithfulness. Simply put, God offered the covenant, and the people experienced its benefits together in a shared life of faith, trust, obedience, gratitude, and generosity.

As we follow the development of the covenant through the Old Testament record, however, we find a long and checkered history. Even though the covenant promised the well-being of God's people, the people did not always *trust* the God of the covenant. Sporadic faithfulness and unfaithfulness characterized the mercurial response of the chosen people to God.

Consider, for example, the story of Moses and the flight of the Hebrew people from Egypt. During their captivity and enslavement in Egypt, the descendants of Abraham were in danger of forgetting their unique identity in relationship with God. Depression, despair, and anger gripped them. Had God forgotten them? Would God save them? In the wilderness, despite Moses' leadership, the people turned from God; they were afraid to trust their safety and well-being in the hands of God. They paid homage to a calf made of gold — a pagan symbol of fortune and prosperity. They even longed for the predictable comforts of slavery in Egypt. Despite these weaknesses and abuses, God continued to draw the people toward a relationship of faith, freedom, and gratitude. Indeed, in keeping with the promises of old, God gave the Ten Commandments at Sinai in order to re-establish a faithful way of life among the people.

Throughout the Old Testament we see a consistent picture of a personal God who seeks a personal relationship with his people in order to help and heal them. However, we also see the people consistently doubting or misinterpreting who God is, disobeying God, losing faith, and, thus, needing a way to be restored to God. Indeed, seen in this light, many of the Old Testament laws related to stewardship themes were given as ways for the people to recover, remember, and reaffirm their faith in God — to be restored to trust in God's faithfulness. Thus, animal sacrifice was instituted not only as a way for the people to acknowledge their sin and unfaithfulness, but also as a way to recognize God's continuing faithfulness, to receive forgiveness, and to pledge renewed commitment. Likewise, tithing was given as a means for the people to remember God's faithfulness. As the people brought their tithes and gave unblemished animals from the best of their stock, they committed themselves again to God's blessings and purposes in covenant and creation.

For this reason, both tithing and sacrifice became part of the worship pattern of ancient Israel. How did one stay in touch with God's faithfulness? How did one respond in order to experience the benefits of the covenant? Faithfulness, joyful obedience, grateful tithing, and committed sacrifice — these were the tried and true responses of the Hebrew tradition.

This same pattern of relationship between God and his people is evident throughout the Old Testament. God longs for a relationship with his people that is faithful through and through. The people lose faith and disobey, yet God remains faithful. In all cases, the focus of restoration and renewal is not simply on outward acts but also on inward dispositions, upon the heart. There is no greater example of such disobedience and restoration than King David. One story in particular shows how David's capacity for genuine giving was crucial to the restoration of his own relationship with God.

In 2 Samuel 24 we find God and David at odds. David wanted to take a census in order to determine the number of persons available for military service and to tax the citizens. His advisors warned him against this lack of trust in God, but David insisted. Later, when Israel suffered a national plague, David realized his sin and asked God what had to be done in order to repent. God directed David to build an altar on the threshing floor of Araunah the Jebusite. When Araunah saw the king approaching his home, he went out to meet David. "Why has my Lord the King come to his servant?" asked Araunah (2 Samuel 24:21). David replied that he had been directed to buy Araunah's threshing floor so that he could make an offering to God as an act of repentance.

Araunah was honored to receive his king, so he offered to give the threshing floor (and all of the other materials needed for the sacrifice) free of charge. "All this, O king, Araunah gives to the king" (2 Samuel 24:23). But David said to Araunah, "No, but I will buy them from you for a price; I will not offer burnt offerings to the Lord my God that cost me nothing" (verse 24). David paid fifty shekels of silver for the threshing floor and the oxen and made his sacrifice to God.

David's attitude and actions showed that his heart had changed toward God. He was once again open to trusting God, hearing God, and receiving God's blessing. As a result, God heard David's supplications, and the plague was removed from Israel.

The Old Testament biblical narrative dramatically reflects God's gracious desire for relationship with his people. The covenant, the law, and the guidelines for offering sacrifices were all given to sustain and restore this relationship. The possibility of the relationship was always a matter of God's initiative and grace, but the relationship was not passive on the human side. Grateful life and joyful obedience were the responses that God desired. First, there was grace; then there was thankful and heartfelt giving as a response to grace. Giving did not *bring* the grace. Giving did not *purchase* grace. Giving was a *response* to grace. Even when the people tried to turn the grace of covenant, law, and sacrifice into something else, God still remained faithful. In the Old Testament, God is a personal God who desires relationship with his people.

JESUS AND HIS FATHER

The God revealed in the Hebrew Scriptures as the God of creation and covenant — who seeks his people in order to free them from bondage and to free them for life — is the same God revealed in the Greek scriptures in the life, teaching, and ministry of Jesus. Regardless of how many times the people misunderstood, misrepresented, and misused the love of God, God remained a God of steadfast love whose will and purpose were the true source and hope of creation. This is why Jesus came teaching about God the Father, made known in the Son, by the power of the Spirit. Jesus' mission was to demonstrate and to fulfill the relational and communal purpose of God in history, to turn people away from self-defensive religion, and to turn them toward the joy of life in the kingdom.

The world seems always to be in search of a savior. The Jews of first-century Palestine were no exception. They longed for one who would come and deliver them. Their messianic expectations took on many different forms, primarily revolving around the Old Testament images of a messianic prophet, priest, or king. Some looked for a Messiah who would place them in positions of power in order to overthrow Rome. Others waited for an apocalyptic teacher who would take them into seclusion away from the evils of the city. Societal pressures and political instability heightened all of these messianic expectations; peaceful times caused a waning of expectation.

Jesus, however, did not come robed in any of the garbs that most of the people were expecting. Jesus was not born as one who would defeat Rome by military force. Nor did he flee to the wilderness. Rather, he was born a defeated Jew, and he publicly engaged the problems of the city. As a result, the world generally greeted him with a lack of hospitality. His birth came in a cold, smelly stable because "there was no room in the inn." Though he was the Messiah, his style did not make sense to the leaders of the day who sought to control people by fear and force. Indeed, by many earthly standards Jesus was simply a failure. We may call him our Lord, but he was a different kind of Lord. Therefore, instead of calling Jesus the expected Messiah, I choose to call him the "unexpected" Messiah.

The scandal of our faith, yet its essence, is the powerless power of the incarnation. God has come to us as an infant in order to reveal again — and as clearly as human life can make possible — who God is: a personal God who seeks a relationship of grace, joy, gratitude, and generosity with us. In the paradox of the infant's powerlessness lies the nature of God. In understanding and responding to God's nature lies our salvation.

Look again at the baby Jesus. As an infant, Jesus was cared for by loving parents. He cried, had to be changed, slept, and ate just as all infants do. God Incarnate, Immanuel, was dependent on Mary and Joseph for his very life. It was they who protected him from Herod's wrath. Lovingly they saw to his needs as a child. God came among us as one who would flourish only in relationship with others.

As an adult, Jesus needed other people. He was not in this world to live and work in a vacuum. The calling of the disciples, as well as the development of the inner and outer circles of followers, speaks of a Messiah who relied on relationships with others. Though they would later abandon him, he did not abandon them. Indeed, he continued to depend upon them and finally committed the future of his own ministry into their hands.

In all of this, Jesus was not inventing a new religion but recovering what he deemed to be the crux of the Old Testament witness. In keeping with his Hebrew scriptures, Jesus taught that joyful obedience is the fitting response to God's goodness and faithfulness. He affirmed that relationship with God is a matter both of deed and heart, and that no matter how low a person may sink, he or she still bears the potential (the *image of God*) for this kind of relationship with God and with others. His parable of the prodigal son echoes the Old Testament witness concerning God's faithfulness to Israel, and applies this to a new generation. In the parable, a father longs for relationship with two estranged children. One son squanders the inheritance. The other covets it. The father extends the *same* invitation to both — the gift of generous and joyful relationship. For Jesus (as for his ancestor, King David), the relationship that God desires is much more than mere outward compliance; it is a matter of joy, trust, and grateful participation.

The prophet Jeremiah had foretold a time when the law would be written on the hearts of the faithful (Jeremiah 31:31-34). The second covenant embodied in Jesus did not nullify the first. Rather, as Jesus himself said, he came to *fulfill* all that God had already given. Thus, the purpose of the first covenant was to bring human beings to health and wholeness by restoring their created relationship with God. Jesus, as the agent of the new covenant, did not reject that purpose; he filled it full of meaning and vitality. Jesus challenged his hearers to allow God's grace and law to be written on their hearts. The law was not given to provoke attitudes of self-righteous comparison and condemnation; it was given to show the way of life with an open heart to God. This way of heart and life was born out of knowing God, trusting God, and following God.

Thus, and again in keeping with the Old Testament heritage, Jesus insisted that matters of stewardship are a window into the heart of our relationship to God. David L. Heetland, in his book, *Fundamentals of Fundraising*, states that Jesus was the greatest stewardship teacher of all. He said more about money than about any other subject, including prayer. In the Gospels, one verse in six focuses on material possessions, and these verses are punctuated with such memorable sayings as, "For where your treasure is, there your heart will be also" (Matthew 6:21); "Give to the emperor the things that are the emperor's, and to God the things that are God's" (Mark 12:17); "From everyone to whom much has been given, much will be required" (Luke 12:48); and "For God so loved the world that he gave his only Son" (John 3:16).[2]

In all of this, Jesus pointed to the joyful economy of God's grace and our giving.

Indeed, Jesus defined joyful obedience primarily in terms of stewardship issues — that is, giving of one's life and resources. According to Jesus, to give joyfully in the manner of a good steward is to get in on life; it is life-giving. Consider, for example, the story of Zacchaeus who went from miserly conduct to generosity all because of Jesus' gracious acceptance. Jesus taught his followers to always remember God's love so that their giving would be transformed from a grudging burden to a joyful duty. The grace-filled relationship one has with God initiates a transformation in how one experiences the act of giving.

Thus, Jesus' frequent focus on issues related to money and possessions did not reflect an obsession. Rather, he simply recognized that money and possessions are a reflection of who a person is. Put another way, money and possessions represent distilled energy. Money takes intangible energy and turns it into something tangible. What we choose to do with our money and possessions reflects our total sense of values. Seen in this light, money and possessions can never be an end in themselves; rather, they are simply a means for faithful service as a steward of God's goodness. Grace precedes giving. As grace-filled children of God, we respond to grace by recognizing that we have been entrusted with much. How we act out our stewardship is a reflection of our reception and awareness of grace from God.

Jesus was not only the great teacher of stewardship, he was its quintessential model. Markus Barth, in an enlightening deviation from traditional designations for Christ, refers to Jesus as "the steward of God."[3] Jesus experienced stewardship just as we are called to do — by trusting in and relying on his relationship with the Father. Barth put it this way: "Jesus Christ is not given a detailed job description. Rather he is trusted to act out freely what pleases the Father."[4]

So it is with all Christians. God in Christ does not coerce faithfulness. Indeed, such would no longer be faith. Rather, God invites faithfulness, always waiting for even the unfaithful with open arms. The relationship with God into which we are invited must be entered in joy, freedom, gratitude, and generosity, if it is to be entered into at all.

The grace-filled relationship that Jesus had with his Father (*Abba*) was full of trust and freedom. Indeed, his trust in the Father was so great that he was finally able to offer his life for the sake of those whom the Father loved. Jesus' death on the cross reflects the depth of the Father's love for the world. The general human suspicion of such grace and love led inexorably to his sacrifice on the cross, but his resurrection from the dead proved the validity of the course that he chose. At the time of his death, even his enemies gave unintentional witness to the consistency of his faith: He "saved others . . . not himself" (Mark 15:31); "Truly this man was God's Son" (Mark 15:39).

Just how far would God go to heal the relationship with human beings? From the moment of creation, God's desire for relationship was evident. Over and again throughout the Old Testament, human suspicion, misapprehension, and rejection did not thwart God's gracious invitation. Then, at the center of history, the Father sent his Son to be a light in the darkness, to shine again even when the shadows appeared to have won. Immanuel, God with us — here is the extent of God's desire to reconcile the world, to restore human beings to right relationship with God, each other, and all of creation. Simply put, God is willing to take our suffering into himself in order to save and heal us; but, like Jesus, we must trust him!

THE HOLY SPIRIT

Thus far, we have focused mainly on the identity of the Father and of the Son. Looking at who God is and what God has done in these ways has shown us much about the joyful and generous meaning of stewardship. Before Jesus ascended, however, he added another promise to the promises of old. He promised to send a helper and a teacher who would draw alongside the disciples, comforting them and empowering them to be witnesses to God's faithful relationship to the whole world. The first disciples certainly needed this kind of help.

Scared, depressed, confused — these are the words that describe the disciples immediately following the crucifixion of Jesus. Jesus had been their cornerstone, their friend. Though he had explained and interpreted what would take place, the disciples lacked understanding. Even when he rose from the dead and appeared to them individually and in groups, they were not sure what to make of his instructions. They were like children whose parents are leaving on a trip. Doubts and questions swirled: "Where are you going? When will you come back? Who is going to take care of us?" Just before he ascended, they asked, "Lord, is this the time when you will restore the kingdom to Israel?" (Acts 1:6). They just did not understand.

Then, on the day of Pentecost, what Jesus had promised took place. The Holy Spirit, the Spirit of Jesus and of his Father, was made manifest with power. Suddenly there was a sound "like the rush of a violent wind" (Acts 2:2). They were filled with power to share the good news. Those listening were able to understand what the disciples were saying. Peter, the uneducated fisherman, changed from a fearful and despondent boaster into a compassionate preacher. People responded to the invitation to have a relationship with God in Christ. Their lives were changed and the church was born.

Peter's message was simple. The promises of God from of old have now been fulfilled in the ministry and resurrection of Jesus the Messiah. The people are once again invited into relationship with the God of the promise. In order to enter into this relationship they must repent (turn around), recognize their need for forgiveness in Christ, and receive the gift of the Holy Spirit (Acts 2:38). No one need be left behind, "For the promise is for you, for your children, and for all who are far away, everyone whom the Lord our God calls to him" (Acts 2:39).

The pattern of creation, covenant, and Jesus' messiahship is now repeated in the promise and ministry of the Holy Spirit. God's faithfulness creates a faithful people. The Spirit brings those who respond to the gospel into a life of solidarity, generosity, gratitude, and joyful living with one another. The writer of Acts says that they met together for teaching and fellowship, shared their possessions with one another "as any had need," and "ate their food with glad and generous hearts" (Acts 2:42-46). Later, when new needs emerged, they appointed special stewards to oversee the distribution of food and the care of widows (Acts 6:1-6). In all of this, the early Christians recognized that their own joy and generosity were gifts of the Holy Spirit, and they grieved for those who "tested the Spirit" by only feigning to trust in the provision of God (Acts 5:1-11).

As a result of the Spirit's presence, moreover, the first disciples (and disciples ever since) became ambassadors of God's relationship to the world. In keeping with all of God's former promises, the gift of the Holy Spirit brought with it an awareness of God's care for all of creation. In the biblical sense, a steward is a person who is in charge of a household. The New Testament uses a Greek word (*oikonomos*) from which our English words *steward* and *stewardship* are derived. The Greek word itself is made up from two other roots — *oikos* meaning "home, dwelling, household, or temple" and *nomos* meaning "law, or principle of management." Thus an *oikonomos* was an overseer, administrator, or fiscal agent for a household. *Oikonomia* is the administration of an estate, household, or temple.

Thus, a steward is not the owner, but rather has been given responsibility for management. Decisions for the management rest solely with the steward. The steward buys and sells goods along with binding or forgiving administrative agreements (Matthew 16:19; 18:18; John 20:23). All of this takes place, moreover, at the behest of the owner and for the benefit of *the household as a whole*. Indeed, as Jesus' parables declare, the owner can be trusted to renounce a bad steward who places the household in jeopardy simply to protect his own claims (Matthew 25:14-30; Luke 12:41-48).

In this light, stewardship is not simply relational; it is *communal* and *global*. In the power of the Spirit, we receive stewardship as a gift, a partnership with God. The kind of kinship that we receive, we are called to pass along to others. And this kinship is not simply an individual relationship. It is also a relationship with the whole people of God. When we receive the Spirit, we become a steward of God's goodness; but we also enter into a relationship with God's people. Together — as the body of Christ — we are stewards of God's generosity to the whole world. What was true for the early church in the power of the Spirit remains true for the church today. Let me illustrate with a more recent story.

I recall hearing the story of a woman who saw a poor, barefoot child roaming the streets of a large city. She took the child by the hand to the closest shoe store. The woman bought the little girl socks and shoes. With "happy feet" the little girl ran gleefully from the store. Disappointed that she had not even received a word of gratitude from the child, the woman paid for the socks and shoes. As she walked out the shop door, the little girl came back to the store, eyes bright with excitement. "Are you God's wife?" she asked the woman. Smiling, the woman said, "No, but I am God's child." The little girl said, "I knew that you were some kin of his." Those who enter into Spirit-filled relationship with God become signs of his kinship to the whole world. This is who God is. This is what God is doing.

A THEOLOGY FOR PREACHING

The trinitarian story of who God is and what God does underscores the relational nature of God's all-encompassing love. In what way are we loved by God? In such a way that God creates us, seeks us out, suffers for and with us, and stays with us in all things. We are invited into this kind of relationship with God and with each other. The relationship is not automatic, for it implies our freedom and response. Yet it is not a burden or drudgery, for it promises our wholeness and healing in the joy and communion for which we are created.

This kind of biblical theology is a theology for head and heart, and it addresses the task of the preacher in at least three ways. First, it suggests that the role of the preacher is to lead the worshiping community in celebrating the relationship into which we are created and for which we are being redeemed. Preaching about stewardship is much more than raising funds; it is an opportunity to respond in freedom and trust to what God has done in Christ. God is in the reconciling business! God was, in Christ, reconciling the world unto himself (2 Corinthians 5:19). Reconciled persons are entrusted and empowered with a ministry of reconciliation. This is what led Isaac Watts to pen the lines of his famous hymn:

> Were the whole realm of nature mine,
> That were an offering far too small;
> Love so amazing, so divine,
> Demands my soul, my life, my all.[5]

Healthy stewardship begins and ends in the praise of God. Who is God? What is God doing? God is our Creator who seeks to restore the relationship for which we are created. God is our kinsman who relates to us as a friend. God is the covenant maker whose covenant promises are *life-giving*. God is the Father who waits for us to come home. God is the Son who, with the Father, welcomes us upon our return.

God is the Spirit who invites us to enter the joy of the Lord and empowers us to share this joy with others. The first privilege of the preacher, therefore, is to lead the people of God in remembering and celebrating God's love.

Second, biblical theology enjoins the preacher to provide opportunities for people to respond in faith to the goodness of God. Who is God? What is God doing? God is the faithful One of Israel who seeks a faithful people to trust him for their needs and future. Such stewardship promises great joy. It also requires placing our trust in God and in others, just as Jesus did. Let me illustrate this by means of a more recent story.

In the late 1890s Blondin was the most famous of all tightrope walkers. His greatest feat was walking across Niagara Falls on a tightrope. Ten thousand people gathered to watch. First he crossed from the Canadian side of the falls to the American side. Everyone was excited and chanted, "Blondin! Blondin! Blondin!" After the crowd was silent, Blondin cried out, "Do you believe in me?" "We believe in you!" the crowd responded. "I will go back across the tight-rope, but this time I will carry someone on my shoulders. Do you believe I can do it?" "We believe! We believe!" answered the crowd. Blondin then asked, "Who will go with me?" The crowd fell silent. Finally out of the 10,000, one stepped forward. He climbed on Blondin's shoulders and for the next three-and-a-half hours Blondin inched his way back to the Canadian side.

Ten thousand shouted that they believed, but only one really believed. Believing is not just giving verbal assent to a propositional statement. Believing is giving one's life without reservation into the hands of the One in whom we believe. This commitment staggers our imaginations! There is a cost to our faith! "Not everyone who says to me, 'Lord, Lord,' will enter the kingdom of heaven, but only the one who *does* the will of my Father in heaven" (Matthew 7:21). Biblical theology compels the preacher to give people opportunities to respond.

This belief in and response to God may come in a variety of ways. For some it is "crisis" driven. Some experience what Søren Kierkegaard called a "leap of faith." Circumstances more or less force some to the point of having to make a decision about following God or not. Others, however, are wooed into God's kingdom. They do not come in "kicking and screaming"; rather, the promise of God's goodness and trustworthiness gradually shapes and wins their commitment. Both models of responding to God can be found in the Old and New Testaments. Ultimately God desires a trusting, free, and confident response — no matter how we come to the point of decision. Preachers who are convinced of God's goodness will give people opportunities to respond.

Third, biblical theology instills in preaching a communal vision for ministry and mission in the wider community and world. Who is God? What is God doing? In view of God's goodness throughout salvation history, preaching eagerly calls the community of faith to take up its role of global stewardship in partnership with God. The thumbprint of God is indelibly etched on human souls, bodies, personalities, and communities. If we really acknowledge this as our true genesis, we must find our role in living out and sharing our faith. God has entrusted to us an awesome gift. We are stewards of the gift of stewardship.

Daniel Kauffman in his book, *Managers with God*, provides a holistic understanding of stewardship within a biblical and theological framework. He writes of Christians as "stewards of the gospel."[6] Christians are entrusted with the gospel and kingdom of God. We are invited to see the world in terms of our partnership with God. To view the world strictly as utilitarian would be to misunderstand the concept of creation and the relational meaning of the incarnation. By contrast, we are co-creators and co-managers with God. To be stewards of the gospel means that we are to continue the work begun by Christ. God uses the voices, personalities, money, and possessions of human beings to communicate with the world. To shirk the responsibility of being a co-creator or co-manager with God means that the kingdom can fall into bad repute. The tragedy for the world and for the church is that the church (like Israel before) has often perverted this responsibility to a preoccupation with saving itself.[7]

In this light, the activity of God — Father, Son, and Spirit — is simply to bring us into the joyful relationship of stewardship that God has promised. Stewardship is not manipulation; rather, it is an invitation for people to look honestly at God, the world, and themselves. When this happens, churches naturally thrive. Transformed by this understanding, the Word becomes good news as opposed to bad news. The powerful story of who God is, and what God has done, is doing, and will do becomes a magnet for people who are searching. Searchers who enter into the joy and privilege of this covenant relationship become ambassadors of God's blessings to all of creation.

4 | THAT WILL PREACH!

One of the phrases we preachers have a tendency to use is, "That will preach." What we mean by that phrase is this: A story, phrase, or incident has just happened or been told to us that we think has possibilities for sharing from the pulpit.

Early in my ministry, an old friend discussed with me the art of thinking and reading from a homiletical perspective. Certainly preachers need to step away from this perspective occasionally, but it remains important nonetheless. As preachers, we have been called by God to look at the world, to live in the world, to be with people, and to interpret all of this from a spiritual perspective. This is not to claim that preachers are the fount of all spiritual insight and knowledge. No one can lay claim to that elevated status. We are, however, fellow travelers who have been called to look at and experience the world through the lens of God's Word.

"That will preach" naturally becomes a part of our jargon when we seek to take our preaching seriously and live with a homiletical perspective. This should never mean that we become separated from the world, simply bystanders watching the world for homiletical insights. Preachers who do this — and the sermons they preach — lack authenticity. Rather, we live, love, laugh, cry, and experience the world like everyone else. When homiletical insights come, we reflect on their meaning and share them with our congregation. If we are on target, the congregation experiences what I call the "Aha! event." The sermon or homiletical illustration opens a door of challenge or insight and the individual responds "Aha!

That is I!" Great preaching always encourages and invites people and congregations to move toward the "Aha! event."

A BETTER WAY: "RIGHT-BRAIN" PREACHING

When we experience something that makes us proclaim "Aha! That is I!", most of the time we are responding in ways that have recently been identified with the "right hemisphere" of the brain. Much has been written about the roles of the left and right hemispheres of the brain. While it is not the purpose of this book to explore that discussion in depth, I believe that the research being done has a profound impact on the way we view the preaching of Jesus, homiletical construction in general, and preaching for giving in particular.

In its most basic form, the "two hemisphere" theory ascribes different functions to each side of the brain. According to recent research, words originate in the left brain. The left hemisphere of the brain "functions in an active, analytic, linguistic way. It gets things done. . . . We can summarize that left hemisphere specialty with considerable confidence: expressive speech, linguistic complexity, propositional cognition, discrete processing, analytical thinking."[1] By contrast, the right hemisphere of the brain is more holistic, relational, and encompassing. Researchers describe right hemisphere functions in terms of "seeing, sensing, feeling, imaging, and singing."[2] Thus, the left brain is more concerned with "doing" while the right brain is more involved with "being."

From the standpoint of this theory, preachers need especially to activate and use the functions of the right hemisphere of the brain. What do I mean? (Certainly not that a preacher needs only half a mind!) Since the vocation of the preacher revolves around words, and words originate in the left brain, no one can legitimately question the importance of left-brain functions in the task of preaching. Nevertheless, in order to hear and communicate words effectively with others, the left hemisphere of the brain must be greatly informed by the right. Further, since preaching at its best is invitational and persuasive, it must also be intuitive, holistic, and global — characteristics that flourish in the images of right-brain awareness.

Biblical evidence of Jesus' actions, personality, and words indicates that he engaged people most often in right-brain ways. To be sure, he at times made simple statements of declaration: ". . . repent, and believe in the gospel" (Mark 1:15*b*). This statement is directive and obligatory; it tells the hearer what to *do*. Such imperative statements show Jesus' capacity for left-brain thinking and left-brain appeals. It is noteworthy, however, that, for the most part, Jesus avoided conversations that tried to persuade by analyzing the fine points of the law (cf. the Scribes and Pharisees). Rather, he helped people picture the kingdom of God, and he invited them to see themselves in the picture. He relied on stories or parables to make his point.[3] With their use of images and feelings, such stories and parables are right-brain centered. Their power owes much to the fact that they leave the crux of interpretation to the listeners.[4]

Why did Jesus use parables and images? Why was his preaching and speaking right-brain focused? Was he intentionally being obscure? Of course not. Jesus was aware that truth and faith can never be given directly. If that were the case, then all Christian parents and grandparents would have children of faith. As we saw in the last chapter (cf. King David and the prodigal son), there is a personal dimension to faith, an inner reality, a "wrestling with God" that every person must experience. A "secondhand" faith that comes through others must finally become a "firsthand" faith. Jesus knew this. Therefore, his preaching was invitational, wooing, openended. He invited unfaithful people to come home, and he waited faithfully for them to do so. Right-brain, invitational preaching relies on God's Holy Spirit to work in the life of the hearer.

Preaching out of the right brain requires the preacher to trust the listener. Two individuals may hear very different things in a given sermon. They may even raise issues on topics which the preacher did not consider as the sermon was written and shared. A phrase, a concept, or a word opens a door in the life of a person, and she or he steps through it. There is no one way that a sermon is heard, understood, or assimilated by different individuals. Thus, preaching at its best is modeled after the concept of Bible story. Hearers are invited to take a journey, hear a story, ask questions, and consider a concept. As the preacher shares the sermon, the hearers may have many different kinds of "Aha! events": "Yes! That is my story, my struggle, my life!" In every "Aha! event" the Holy Spirit is at work.

PREACHING FOR GIVING USING THE RIGHT BRAIN

Preaching for giving is greatly affected by the degree to which sermons engage the energies of the right hemisphere of the brain. Jesus most often invited people to consider the nature of their stewardship before God by means of parables (right-brain preaching). He helped them envision the radical commitment of discipleship, and he implicitly encouraged them to join the movement of God's kingdom. Consider how different things would have been had Jesus presented salvation and faithful living simply as external concepts or behaviors (left brain), something simply to be defined and checked rather than a vision to pursue.

Many laypersons and preachers with good intentions ask mainly left-brain kinds of questions: "Have you been saved?" "Are you saved?" Biblically and theologically, these questions are helpful, but they are not sufficient in themselves. They must be augmented with another question: "Are you being saved?" Or, in more Wesleyan language, "Are you going on to perfection?" From this angle, faith is more of a right-brain process than a left-brain event!

Look at Peter, the disciple. His conversion was a process! First, he was called by Jesus to be a fisher of men and women (Matthew 4:18-19). This was a time of moral transformation. Peter made the decision to follow Jesus. Second, he was converted after failure. Turning his back on Jesus, Peter denied him three times (Matthew 26:57-75). Third, he was converted from his old life. After the Resurrection, Peter went back to fishing (John 21:3-19)! He retreated to safety and security. Jesus had to call him back to service. Fourth, as the early church grew and spread, Peter was converted from his prejudice and bigotry (Acts 10). He was forced to deal with the fact that all people are children of God.

Process, intuition, invitation, feeling, and sensing — these are functions of the right brain. These are the functions that Jesus emphasized in his preaching; but does our preaching for giving take this into account? *Sadly, I think many of us approach our financial stewardship sermons only from the left brain.* Our words indicate that giving is obligatory. The tone we use is condemning. Even the body language and posture we exhibit in the pulpit indicate how totally uncomfortable we feel with preaching for giving. The congregation senses that something is wrong. They walk away from traditional stewardship sermons feeling "whipped" and guilty. Is it any wonder, then, that the word *stewardship* has taken on negative connotations with clergy and laity? We have taken a great biblical word, *stewardship*, and through misuse, abuse, and manipulation robbed it of its invitational power to joyful and holy living.

Many preachers have unintentionally fallen into the trap of preaching judgmental, puritanical, obligatory, left-brain stewardship sermons. Nothing else has been modeled for them. Therefore, with some fear and trepidation, I wish to offer two sermons in which I try to model the principles I have been describing. Naturally, I offer these as "models" only in the sense of a shared journey, not in the sense of attainment. Along with this qualification, moreover, I wish to add three suggestions about how to use these models.

First, insofar as possible, translate these literary models into an oral setting. Preaching of the kind that I wish to recommend is an oral process — not a literary event. Preaching paints a picture on a canvas of time. Spoken words ride a wave of sound and echo in the rhythm of immediate memory. Hearers interact with the visual as well as with the auditory presence of the speaker. Themes repeat. Images combine. Tone of voice changes. Feelings shift. Insights emerge in unpredictable ways — for both preacher and hearers. It is difficult to translate such a process infused by God's Spirit into the far more fixed and linear medium of the printed page. Much simply does not survive the passage. Therefore, translate to the oral setting.

Second, use these models as a springboard for your own creativity. Preaching of the kind that I wish to recommend is a creative process. Preaching, like life, is full of ambiguity. Sermons spring from the dynamic interplay of all that we hope and all that we suffer. No human activity, including preaching, can (or should try to) remove the dynamic character of life itself. Fortunately, the kind of giving that God desires is born out of joyful response to the promise and faithfulness of God, not out of reducing life to rigid rules or controls. My goal has not been to craft a set of irreproachable sermons, but to try to follow Jesus in opening a window onto the joyful economy of God's grace and our giving. Therefore, be creative and don't worry about absolute consistency.

Third, translate the personal aspect of these models into your own congregational setting. You will find very specific references to situations and people. I have let these stay in the sermons with the permission of those mentioned. Not all sermons need to be so specific, but if sermons are truly to connect the vision of God's grace with the joy of the people's giving, they must be timely and pertinent to the local congregation. Therefore, as you consider these models, keep the people of your congregation in mind.

Model 1: I SAW SATAN FALL
(Luke 10:1-12, 17-20)

I am convinced that one of the things that makes us truly human is our struggle with despair. Every single one of us, if we are honest, wonders what kind of difference we make in the world. Ultimately, when you get right down to it, what kind of difference do we make?

What is despair? It is trying to talk with our children, yet not feeling like we are getting through. We want to throw up our hands and say, "I'm not going to make any difference. What difference do the words that I say make in their lives?" Or we may have a friend at work with whom we have been trying to share and talk for many months or years. That facade over her or his person, over her or his demeanor, has not been broken and our witness seems to have fallen on deaf ears. We want to know, "What difference do I make? What difference does my witness make?"

Despair is also a part of church life. We bring in food for outreach ministries. We feed a few families. We build a home for someone who has been living in substandard housing. However, when we deal with the issue of world hunger, what difference does it make what we do? We certainly are not going to solve the problem of world hunger. We think, "Why do anything at all? It is not going to make any difference." When we think about the thousands of people who will die of starvation this coming week, when we think about the housing issue, what difference does it make? We have not even made a dent in it. What difference does it make?

Jesus struggled with despair. You may be surprised to hear me say that. This man was 100 percent divine and 100 percent human. To be human means to struggle with despair. I think of how he struggled at times with people. He would grow weary and wonder, "What difference does it make?" How would he react during those times? The Bible tells us that he would get into a boat and escape to the other side of the lake, just to get away from people. Or maybe he would go to a mountain, just to be away from people. It was his desire to grow strong again; but also, there was a threat of despair with which he was struggling. He knew it deep down in his soul. "What difference does it make what I do?" was also his question.

Then I think about Jesus' struggle with despair in the Garden of Gethsemane. He knelt, prayed, and said, "God, I'm not sure that I can go through with this. Please let me avoid this, if at all possible. Let this cup pass from me." This was Jesus' struggle with despair.

Finally there can be no more powerful question of despair than the one asked by Jesus as he hung on the cross. "My God, my God, why have you forsaken me?" ("Where are you God? I am dying here. Where are you God? Have I died for nothing?")

Jesus knew what it meant to despair. He struggled with the same emotions as you and I. What difference does it make what we do? What difference does it make what witness we make? What difference are we making in the world? Are we even making a dent? Are we really changing anything? What difference does it make?

The events reported in the tenth chapter of Luke are important for the church to hear, I believe, because they deal specifically with the issue of despair. Jesus had called seventy of his followers together. They are described by Luke as disciples. Jesus said, "Listen, I am going to send you out; I am going to give you power; I want you to touch the lives of people. I am going to be moving into these villages behind you before too long. I want you to go on ahead of me."

How do you think these seventy people received Jesus' commission? Do you think they jumped up and said, "Fantastic, we really are excited about this. We are going to make a difference in this world." Probably not; after all, they were persons like you and I. They asked the same questions you and I would have asked: "How are we going to get along? Will we be safe? Will we make a difference? What if our abilities are not adequate?" Jesus' instructions — take no extra provisions, stay with those who receive you — show that he was answering these kinds of worries. So, the seventy went out. Jesus told them to eat in the homes of the people, to witness, to heal people, and to proclaim to listeners that the kingdom of God was at hand. That was his directive to them.

Do you know what happened when the seventy went out? They went out with doubting spirits; they came back energized. They went out wondering, "What's going to happen? You know, I'm just plain old Joe. What am I going to do to touch the lives of people?" They went out with anxiety, but they went out. And they came back empowered. They discovered to their surprise that when they spoke, they spoke with power, and when they healed, they healed with power, and when they witnessed, they witnessed with power.

Upon returning to Jesus the disciples said, "Jesus, even the demons were subject to us through the power of your name!" Jesus laughed and said, "I know, I know. I felt the power, too. For as you were doing your work, I saw Satan fall like lightning from heaven." (That is to say, "I saw evil going down to defeat because of the good works you were doing.")

What difference does it make what we do? It makes all the difference in the world for those with whom we are sharing. When I think about this passage of scripture, do you know who comes to mind? I think about Joe and Eden Christopher. They are a part of our church, active members of our church. Joe works at Georgia Power. The Christophers have a little boy, Kevin, who has had medical difficulties since birth. Insurance has taken care of most of the expenses. However, as you know, it never takes care of everything. They have had so many expenses with this little boy that it has been a real struggle for them financially and emotionally.

Several months ago Eden and Joe realized that they needed to go to Massachusetts to a hospital where there was a specialist who worked with children like Kevin. Eden and the children traveled to Boston, and Joe stayed here. He needed to work and could not afford to go with his family. One of you became aware of that situation and felt that Joe needed to fly up for a weekend to be with his family. You started talking among yourselves. Sunday school classes were contacted. Before long, all of this caring and sharing had translated itself into a round-trip plane ticket for Joe Christopher. After he got word of the ticket, he called me. "Tim, you will never know what this means to me. This is so special. This means more to me than you will ever know, and I am grateful for the people of Martha Bowman Church and what they are enabling me to do." As I heard Joe Christopher say those words, *I saw Satan fall like lightning from heaven*.

Several weeks ago Delia Steffen was consecrated as a diaconal minister. She is full-time staff with us here. What a special, powerful service that was. Many of you were present. I looked around at that service, and I saw your smiling faces and your desire to be supportive of Delia and her ministry. Here was a young woman who had given herself to God. She has already made an impact on us as people of God at Martha Bowman Church. As the years unfold, there will be hundreds, even thousands, of people she will touch, and lives will be changed as a result of her witness. As I participated in worship with Delia, *I saw Satan fall like lightning from heaven*.

What difference does it make what we do? We can make all the difference in the world to those who are searching. What power we have in our hands! Not our own power, mind you, but the power of Jesus, the power of the Holy Spirit. When we despair or, worse, become cynical, we need to hear this word from the tenth chapter of Luke saying that it really does matter what we do. It really does! Sometimes we may be able to do things for one group of people and at the same time see hundreds of thousands and even millions of people who need to have the same thing done for them. "What difference does it make? I have not changed anything." In the midst of that, Jesus looks at us and says, "As you do what you do, as you share in ministry, as you share in mission, I see Satan falling like lightning from heaven."

Those of you who were here several weeks ago will remember that I told the story of my encounter with a little boy in our church. I am going to tell it again because I want to tell you what happened as a result of the story.

One Sunday morning I was worn out and tired, emotionally drained, physically exhausted, as I am after three services of worship. After worship there are always several people with whom I need to meet. In the midst of those meetings, Tim Steffen, my associate, came to me, and said, "Tim, there is a migrant family in the office, and they need some help." In an exasperated tone of voice I said, "You handle it. Give them some money out of petty cash and send them on their way if you will. Take care of the situation. I do not have the time or energy to deal with them." I had important things to do and people I needed to see.

When I made my way to the office, the migrant family was still there. They recognized me as a minister of the church. The father said, "Thank you for what you have done." (We had only given them a small amount of cash to send them on their way.) The little boy looked at me and said, "Do you have any toys around?" Once again, I had so many things to do.

With a sigh of exasperation, I looked at Tim as if to say, "Get this kid off my back!" Tim found a balloon for the boy. The boy said, "I get very tired riding in the car all day long. I don't have anything to do." In the midst of all that, I went into my office and shut the door and met with the "important" church people.

Later that week, the name of the boy dawned on me. His name was "Jesus." There I was in the midst of my "important" church business. I needed to drop everything I was doing and go and buy a coloring book and some crayons or a puzzle. But no, I had "important" church business that demanded my attention.

As a result of hearing me tell this story, a woman in our congregation called the church office and said, "I want to do something to solve that problem." She put together packets of material that we have in the church office now — packets for both older kids and younger kids — coloring books, crayons, puzzles and the like, things kids can do in the car. She expressed her desire to be of service in this way (a specific, hands-on, where-the-rubber-meets-the-road kind of way). As she shared with the staff what she wanted to do, as she carried out that ministry, *I saw Satan falling like lightning from heaven*. What difference does it make? It makes all the difference in the world to those we are called to touch.

Margaret Gordon is here this morning, bless her. Stewart Gordon, Margaret's husband, died about four or five weeks ago. He was a patriarch in this church. What a lovely person, lovely personality. He struggled with the debilitating emotional and physical effects of a serious stroke. You will remember him as an elderly man who struggled to get around the church. But he was here, struggling. When I went to visit Margaret right after Stewart died, she said to me, "I don't see how anybody can go through times like this if they are not a part of a church community." That stuck in my mind. You see, I knew that you and I were acting out God's love in specific ways:

taking food, sending a card, or praying. Margaret felt that, as well as Ellen and John, the children in the family. As Margaret told me she did not feel anybody ought to have to go through something like this without the support of the Christian community, *I saw Satan fall like lightning from heaven.*

What difference does it make — bringing a jar of peanut butter or some dried beans or some corn meal to put in a basket for Macon Outreach? What difference does it make, building a home for Habitat? What difference does it make to contact Paul and Carol Smith about upcoming surgery? What difference does it make that we support missionaries or give money to support missions and outreach around this world? Are we simply throwing away money? What difference does it make?

What difference does it make if we visit in the homes of people who have a death in their families? What difference does it make if we show up in the hospital or make a phone call or send a card? What difference does it make? When we get to feeling like that, we need to look once again at this story in Luke. Jesus told those seventy disciples, "Be with the people, feed the people, heal the people, be in their homes, show them that the kingdom of God is at hand." When they came back they said, "Jesus, we cannot believe it. We had power; we were even able to cast out demons through the power of your name." And Jesus looked at them and said, "I know, I know. I felt the power, too. I saw Satan fall like lightning from heaven."

Jesus looks at all the things we do. Sometimes we despair. What difference does it make? What difference do I really make in this world? As we are involved in ministry, mission, and outreach, Jesus looks at us very specifically as people of God at Martha Bowman Church and says to us, "As you do your good works, as you share in the mission, *I see Satan falling like lightning from heaven!*" Thanks be to God.

Model 2: COME TO A WRESTLING MATCH
(Genesis 32:24-30)

Several weeks ago while watching television, I came across a show I had never seen, entitled, "Gorgeous Ladies of Wrestling." Feeling that it was important to know what was going on in the world, I watched with fascination as the "Gorgeous Ladies" did battle. Our eight-year-old was equally amazed at what was taking place. We were fine until my wife walked through the room. This show is now off limits for us.

That show brought back memories for me. One of the organizations at Metter High School needed to raise money, so they hosted a wrestling match. It was the first time I had seen "pro" wrestling. There were little people wrestling, women wrestling, and men wrestling. There was a good guy and a bad guy in every single one of those wrestling matches. The crowd was yelling and talking to the entertainers. I realized, of course, that it was all choreographed and pre-determined. The entertainers knew the exact moves to make and the holds to put on each other. It was like watching a drama unfold.

Today I want to invite you to a wrestling match. In fact, you are invited to two wrestling matches. Neither one of these wrestling matches was or is predetermined. In the first wrestling match, you will find on my left in the ring, Jacob, who is the son of Isaac and Rebekah. Jacob is a schemer and a plotter par excellence, for he is the one who robbed his brother, Esau, of a birthright. On the other side of the ring is God Almighty, the Creator of the world. How is it that Jacob found himself in a wrestling match with God Almighty? What good does it do to wrestle with God? How can one presume to wrestle with God? This is the predicament in which Jacob found himself.

Jacob was a gifted young lad. From his earliest days he was always plotting and scheming as to how to get more. He wanted to control his destiny. Jacob had a way of manipulating people so that he always won. One of the persons he manipulated was Esau, his brother. Jacob disguised himself to look like Esau, and at his father's deathbed extracted from Isaac the birthright which rightfully belonged to Esau. In the midst of Jacob's dishonesty, Esau became so upset that he threatened to kill Jacob. Jacob fled in fear to another land. There, because of manipulative efforts and charisma, he became a very wealthy person. However, his soul was empty. This emptiness in Jacob's soul was due to the fact that he was estranged and separated from his brother, Esau. He knew he had done wrong.

Not knowing what the future held, Jacob set out for the land where Esau was living. He did not know if Esau would try to kill him. With faith he sought to straighten out his relationship with the person he had wronged. One night Jacob camped by the river Jabbok. While he was there, a person came walking through the camp. Jacob was attacked and wrestled all night with the unknown traveler. Jacob was strong and tried to get the advantage, but this traveler, this stranger, was stronger. Eventually Jacob realized that he was wrestling with God Almighty. God finally pinned Jacob and said: "Jacob, I'm going to change your name. No longer am I going to call you Jacob. From now on your name will be Israel."

The next morning Jacob awoke with pain because his hip had been thrown out of joint in the wrestling match. Jacob realized that he had been in the presence of God. He continued the journey to Esau's home. Upon seeing Jacob, Esau opened his big arms and said, "Come here, little brother." They ran together and hugged. Jacob said to Esau, "When I look into your face, I feel as though I am seeing the face of God."

Wrestling. Now it is time for the second match. We watched Jacob and God wrestle, and God won that wrestling match. But the interesting thing is that in losing to God, Jacob actually won in another way, because he found the opportunity to reconcile himself to Esau and to make his life full and whole.

In the second match, on my left, in the corner of the ring, is you. And on my right, in the other corner of the ring, is God Almighty. In that ring, I find myself. I am being invited by God to wrestle with God. Do you feel the same kind of fear that I feel when I think about wrestling with God? Who am I to wrestle with God? How do you wrestle with God? How do you get a grip on God? How does God get a grip on you? What does it mean to wrestle with God? I believe that the primary way we as Christian individuals wrestle with God is with our pocketbooks.

What is your definition of money? Let me tell you my definition. Money is distilled energy. When we work, we do not have the ability to touch the energy we are giving as we work. It is intangible. However, it comes back to us in the form of symbols. The primary symbol that we have to reflect our energy is money. Money is not inherently evil. That is neither an Old Testament nor a New Testament concept. What we do with money and the way we allow ourselves to be molded and shaped by money can be evil — even catastrophic. It can create a crisis in our lives. But money, in itself, is not evil. It is not dirty or filthy. What are we to do with money? How are we to talk about money?

The primary way we wrestle with God is with money. Money can be good if used for the glory of God. When we withhold our finances from God, we are withholding our energy. We are withholding ourselves. Money has no value apart from what it represents. What makes it valuable is that it represents who we are, what we have done.

Many of us have refused to wrestle with God. Our giving patterns are abysmal. The average United Methodist gives 1.75 percent of his or her income to God's work. Giving at this level means that we are climbing out over the ropes to avoid wrestling with God.

Once, while Jacob was sleeping, he saw a vision, a dream. In this dream there was a ladder. This ladder stretched from heaven to earth. On the ladder were angels who were ascending and descending. When he awoke, Jacob said, "I know that I have been in the presence of God." He named the place where he had this dream, "Bethel." Jacob said, "From now on because of what God had done for me I choose to give back a tenth of what I have to the work of God."

Tithing is frightening for many of us. In taking this step we climb into the wrestling ring. It represents an act of commitment. For Jacob, tithing was a response to God's blessing. So it is with us. Being a part of God's kingdom means wrestling with God and asking hard questions: "God, how do you want to use me? What do you want to do with me, God? How do you want to use my distilled energy? How do you want to use my money, God?"

Money is neither filthy nor inherently evil nor inherently dirty. It reflects who we are before God. How we use money is a symbol of how we feel about God. I invite you to come to a wrestling match. The first match has already been finished. Jacob and God wrestled. Jacob lost that wrestling match. But in losing the wrestling match, Jacob won the rest of his life. Now it is time for the second match. God is standing in the ring waiting for us. Trembling, we climb into the ring. We wrestle with God. We wrestle with our distilled energy. God will win this wrestling match. When God wins the wrestling match with us, we are the ultimate winners, because we are made into a new creation.

CONCLUDING REFLECTIONS

How do these sermons model right-brain preaching? Images are the key. Both sermons depend on images to aid the hearer in responding to the Word. Let's look at this in a bit more detail.

In the first sermon, "I Saw Satan Fall," I drew from traditional African-American preaching in setting up the cadence. Cadence, songs, poetry, and choruses are right-brain processes. While reading this pericope from Luke 10, I was struck by the verbal and visual image of "Satan falling like lightning from heaven." That metaphor is right-brain focused. Many great African-American preachers have taken a universal experience, wrapped that experience in a right-brain image, and used a cadence to set the tone for their sermon. Dr. Martin Luther King Jr.'s most famous sermon, "I Have a Dream," does just exactly this. With passion and love he proclaims numerous times in the sermon, "I have a dream." A whole nation responded to this powerful moment of persuasion and invitation. That right-brain sermon is a defining moment for the Civil Rights movement. It is a watershed event for our nation.

The sermon, "I Saw Satan Fall," is my attempt to name a universal human experience (that is, despair or cynicism), and then to let the right-brain biblical image speak. First, I acknowledged the human problem: We can be paralyzed by despair or cynicism. These are emotions that, I believe, have been present as long as humans have been on the earth. Second, I asked the question, "What are we to do about such feelings?" Using biblical imagery, I tried to imagine what the seventy must have felt as they were sent out by Jesus. They came back from their journey recognizing that they had made a difference. Jesus, using his typical right-brain response, stated, ". . . I saw Satan fall like lightning from heaven."

From there I attempted to say to my congregation that what they do matters. I sought to be specific in my listing of situations where they had made a difference. Vulnerability is a part of this sermon in that I shared an instance when I was not sensitive to a little boy who needed my attention and help. Throughout the sermon I kept coming back to the chorus: *"I saw Satan fall like lightning from heaven!"*

My second sermon relies on a Bible story to create the right-brain image. Jacob modeled the best and the worst of human nature. His life was not one of righteous piety. The wrestling match of Genesis 32 is the story of God getting a hold on Jacob. Is that not every person's story? Coming to grips with the implications of faith and responding to God's call is a wrestling match for most of us. Relational theology based on the incarnation reminds us that God has come into the world to wrestle with all of us. The event of the incarnation means that we are confronted with a Savior who loves, challenges, and disturbs us. We "wrestle" with this God, asking questions, such as, "How do I live?" "How do I give?" "How do I respond?"

My goal in both of these sermons is to bring the members of my congregation to the place where each of them can declare, "Aha! That is I!" How well do I succeed? That could only be answered in many different ways by seeing into the hearts and minds of the hearers. Insofar as the hearers are able to make the connection among the biblical image, the sermon, and their own experiences, the sermons succeed. To that extent I receive the great privilege of participating in a process whereby the words of the sermon become the Word of God. Thanks be to God.

5 | SOME COMMON PITFALLS

Old habits are hard to break. Those of us who preach are particularly susceptible to this truism. We get it in our minds that the way we have done things in the past is the way we should keep doing things in the future. How difficult it is for God's fresh and alive Spirit to capture our souls and cause us to refocus our attention and preaching.

Some of us need to have a conversion experience related to our preaching for giving. We have fallen into habits that are unhealthy for us as preachers and are deadly for the advancement of God's kingdom. In this chapter I want to explore some of those common pitfalls. They fall into four categories: ignoring the market, attacking the market, misinforming the market, and silence in the pulpit.

IGNORING THE MARKET

Referring to our congregations as "the market" sounds crass. They are God's children! But the reality is that they are the market for our preaching and witness. We have a gospel we want to share with them. God called us to preach and has equipped us for the task of sharing the good news with our market. As I listen to many sermons, however, I notice that few preachers pay attention to their market. The sermons they preach are generic in nature. There is no specificity which indicates that the sermon was prepared for this particular congregation.

Matthew, Mark, Luke, and John did not write generic Gospels. They were all evangelists and preachers. Their sole purpose in writing was to convince their community, their market, that Jesus was and is Lord. It was not their goal to write a chronological history of the life of Jesus. If that was their purpose, then they did a poor job. Even the synoptic Gospels (Matthew, Mark, and Luke) disagree at points over certain aspects of the chronology of Jesus' life. Why did Mark not mention the birth narratives? Why do Matthew and Luke focus on the birth narratives? Why did the Apostle Paul (who wrote many of his epistles prior to the Gospels) focus his writings around the cross and resurrection rather than the birth?

The ancient writers made decisions about what to include in their writings based on the needs and problems of their markets. Each one had a different and unique community. Matthew, for example, begins his Gospel with a recitation of genealogy. This was evidently important to Matthew's market, a Jewish community. The first step in proving Jesus to be the Messiah in a first-century Jewish community was to show his family connection to King David. Jesus was a descendant of David. Accepted prophecy indicated that the Messiah would come from David's line. Matthew knew his market.

John's Gospel, by contrast, would have raised more questions than it answered in Matthew's community. John wrote with an emphasis on questions that were important to his more Hellenistic market. John includes no genealogy; there are no birth narratives. Rather, he begins with the importance of Jesus' ministry in the order of creation. The first step in proving Jesus to be the unique representative of God for a first-century Hellenistic community was to show his connection with the meaning and purpose of the cosmos. Thus, John boldly proclaimed that Jesus, the Messiah, was also the Word (logos) made flesh. John knew his market.

The Gospel writers and Paul knew and cherished the basic chronological history of Jesus' life, ministry, death, and resurrection. Their interest in this history, however, exceeded the recitation of past events. More accurately, they were interested in how this history addressed the present and the future of the people to whom they preached. Therefore, each writer looked closely at the community being addressed and sought to "take every thought captive" for the sake of Christ (2 Corinthians 10:5). Their markets were not the same. As a consequence, neither were their writings. Though the writers used different twists and emphases, all of them nonetheless spoke truthfully of the same Lord. In the Gospels and Pauline epistles, we have some very good models of how to preach to particular markets.

Market research is not easy. For the most part, our markets as preachers are our congregations, and each congregation is different. Some congregations are younger, some older. Some are poorer, some wealthier. Some are more educated, some less. To whom are we preaching? How do we focus and fine-tune a sermon that will be heard by a particular market?

Creativity is crucial. We preachers must avoid the seductive trap of pulling all of our thoughts from someone else's work! Ben Franklin tells the story of a young Presbyterian preacher he admired for his powerful preaching. However, there were those who disapproved of the young man's oratory. Franklin defended his young preacher friend. One of the adversaries heard a sermon preached by the young preacher and thought he had heard it before. Sure enough, the young preacher told Franklin that none of the sermons he preached were his own. "His memory was such as enabled him to retain and repeat any sermon after one reading only." Franklin's comment: "I stuck by him, however, as I rather approved of his giving us good sermons composed by others, than bad ones of his own manufacture. . . ."[1] At this point I disagree with Benjamin Franklin.

Markets and congregations can forgive many things. How long-suffering most of our congregations are! But lack of love is not an easily excusable offense. Poor preparation and no creativity smack of lack of love and caring. Why do we not love or care enough to prepare for our market? If the gospel is a weighty matter, if we believe that it has unmatched gravity, then why do we spend so little time preparing for its proclamation? When we borrow too freely and avoid doing creative homework, our souls crumble in the pulpit. Our market knows what is happening. They see and sense the lack of authenticity. Graciousness on their part prevents them from speaking to us about our preaching. It is hard for them to challenge their preacher and pastor.

The problem with borrowing too much has more to do with meeting real needs than with plagiarism per se. To be sure, plagiarism (borrowing without acknowledgment) is a serious problem. The greatest loss, however, is that of missing the opportunity to address the needs of our congregations authentically and creatively. Like the writers of the Gospels, we should design our sermons to speak specifically to our markets. Is the gospel that important? You bet it is! Is preaching for giving that weighty? Yes!

In both of the right-brain sermons modeled above (pages 59-60), I referred specifically to people, events, and issues that were relevant to my local congregation. In another congregation these specific references would have made no sense. When I spoke certain names, or recalled a particular circumstance, the members of the congregation were able to resonate with me because these were their friends. There was a sense of corporate ownership of the stories. The specificity in the sermons strengthened the bond between pastor and people. These sermons were not written in a vacuum. In a sense, they did not even belong to me. The congregation, God's Spirit, and I working together gave rise to these sermons. The ability of the members to hear the Word was strengthened by their awareness in the sermon of having already been heard. We are mistaken when we think of the pulpit as a place for monologue. Preaching is dialogue. How can we articulate concerns within the context of the Word if we have not heard our people?

Get to know your market. Listen to them. Eat with them. Pray and worship with them. Laugh and cry with them. When this happens, you, the preacher, will know your market. Your sermons will flow from your soul. The market will react with support because they will feel loved. Even with an imperfect, blemished sermon there will be a connection, because the sermon is a labor of love. Congregations and markets respond to love.

ATTACKING THE MARKET

We preachers sometimes carry a big chip on our shoulders. The call to preach creates within us a pharisaical cancer. Invulnerable piety grows out of self-righteousness. Proclamation becomes an opportunity to attack, chastise, or beat up on the congregation. We are the dispensers of the Word. No one present knows the Word better. If we perceive anyone questioning us, we give them the impression they are attacking God. In short, it is possible to view our congregations, our markets, as adversaries. Those who relate to their markets in this manner use the pulpit to hide their own insecurities.

Preaching for giving is particularly susceptible to attacking the market. I once heard a preacher say to the members of his congregation that if they did what they ought to do financially, then he would never have to preach one of these awful stewardship sermons again. That sermon lacked hope, redemption, and invitation. It attacked the congregation.

When we get caught up in attacking the market, we usually use guilt as our weapon. There is a sense of "ought-ness" and obligation to our preaching. Our sermons become heavy-handed and puritanical in nature. Judgmentalism is our hallmark. I contend that our culture in general and our

congregational markets in particular do not respond well
to guilt as a motivating tool. In a society where everyone is
free to "take it or leave it," people simply walk away from
heavy-handed pressure. More important, Jesus' style was
not focused around the promotion of guilt. On the contrary,
Jesus sought to free people from guilt. Jesus did, however,
challenge his market.

*There is a big difference between challenging the market
and promoting guilt.* When the preacher challenges the
market, she or he is inviting the listener to consider the
implications of the good news. Sometimes the implications
mean that the challenge is not easy. Ramifications of the
challenge may be painful. But the challenge is issued out of
love. It is an invitation rather than an attack. Our markets
can tell the difference between invitational challenges and
guilt-ridden attacks. Consider, for example, the story of
Zacchaeus.

When Jesus came to Jericho, he met Zacchaeus, an
individual who had abused people by using his power to tax
(Luke 19). It would have been easy for Jesus to lambaste
Zacchaeus, burdening him with guilt and obligation. Not
one time did Jesus verbally tell Zacchaeus what he ought to
do. Jesus' presence did, however, challenge Zacchaeus, and
Zacchaeus responded in a manner that was specifically financial. Jesus' presence and invitation caused the change. The
metamorphosis was reflected in monetary terms. If Jesus had
used this opportunity to attack, what do you think Zacchaeus
would have done? I believe that Zacchaeus would never have
responded. Jesus knew his market.

There were times, of course, when Jesus' invitations were
rejected. Consider, for example, the story of the rich young
adult in Mark 10:17-27. In many ways, this young man was
the ancient counterpart of a modern-day yuppie. He had
heard of Jesus whose reputation was spreading all over
Palestine. Jesus was known as a great teacher and preacher,

and there were rumors that he was even performing miracles.
Being a young aristocrat, and moving up in society, the young
man no doubt wanted to be "with it," so he went to hear Jesus.

Picture this young man dressed for the occasion in his
best Hart, Schaffner, and Marx $500 suit, wearing a silk tie,
a starched white shirt just back from the cleaners, and
Johnston and Murphy shoes. Picture him driving in his
BMW to the place where Jesus was scheduled to appear.
According to the Gospel account, Jesus had to deal on that
occasion with an unruly crowd — deflecting the trick question of a religious opponent, and welcoming children to the
inner circle of his followers. No doubt the first-century
yuppie was thoroughly impressed with how cool, smart, and
caring Jesus seemed to be.

When Jesus finished teaching and preaching, the crowd
dispersed, but the yuppie did not rush away. Despite his
BMW and his comfortable lifestyle, something was evidently
gnawing at him. He wanted to talk further with Jesus about
the meaning and point of life. His question was timeless and
universal: "Master, what must I do to inherit eternal life?"

We are familiar with the rest of the story. Jesus engaged
the young man in conversation and gradually took his
measure. First Jesus pointed to the importance of the commandments, but the young man apparently felt no need in
that department. Then Jesus refocused the issue at a level
specifically suited to the young man's need: "You lack one
thing. Go and sell all that you have, give it to the poor, and
follow me." The young man felt the wallet in his pocket
and walked away shaking his head, perhaps with a trace of
sadness in his eyes. He opened the door of his BMW, got
inside, cranked up the car, put it in gear, and drove off.

Had we been present among the disciples, what might
have been our response? I can imagine their frustration.
Why had Jesus let this one slip away? This man had potential.
Had Jesus been too demanding? Had he scared the young

man off? As preachers, we know how tempting it can be to soften the demands of the gospel, but we also know how difficult it can be to watch someone walk away.

As I reflect on this passage, I like to think that the disciples learned something from Jesus that day. Perhaps when they turned back to him in frustration they saw something else in his eyes — a sad yet knowing concern about the condition of the young man's heart, including his motives for giving. Instead of trying to take advantage of the immediate situation, Jesus had placed a challenge before the man, a vision for a new way of living. I have a feeling that somewhere down the road this rich yuppie did not finally outrun the challenge and invitation of Jesus. When I get to heaven, I want to talk with that yuppie about the times when I have heard Jesus' challenge, only to find myself reticent to follow. Thank God that my reluctance, like that of the young man, does not make the invitation cease. Thank God for his tenacity in issuing invitations and challenges!

The story of Jesus and the young man is another example of a right-brain story that will preach. Following the example of Jesus, preachers can learn to proclaim right-brain sermons that recognize salvation as a process and leave open the possibility of God's future work in the lives of individuals. In doing this, preachers can and certainly will issue the challenge of discipleship; but they can do this without having to attack their markets. Preaching for giving should not and must not be used as an occasion to attack the market. Chastising tones will only alienate those who need to hear the life-giving Word. The author of Second Timothy states our task this way: ". . . be straightforward in your proclamation of the truth" (2 Timothy 2:15b, NEB). As preachers, we invite and challenge. We then trust God's Spirit to work in the lives of those who are our market. In issuing a challenge or invitation, one has to leave the response in the hands of the listener.

MISINFORMING THE MARKET

Preachers of genuine stewardship have to live down certain images in our culture. Several years ago God decided to perform an act of terrorism by holding Oral Roberts hostage. Roberts told the television audience that if his ministry did not receive a certain amount of money within a specified period of time, he would die. This appeal over the air waves insinuated that God was in the hostage-taking business. In a similar vein, Jim Bakker was arrested, tried, and convicted of fraud for misuse of funds he had solicited over his PTL television program. His opulent lifestyle made us cringe, for we knew that his abuse of church funds would make it more difficult to have credibility as Christian pastors. Some individuals and groups have drawn the conclusion that all Christian pastors must be like Jim Bakker and Oral Roberts.

While I am keenly aware that the above two examples are extremes, they serve to point to a third pitfall for us as we preach for giving. Sometimes we fall into the insidious trap of misinforming our market. We use erroneous theology and manic manipulation to try and motivate our congregations. When you think about it, Roberts' contention is ludicrous. It is not within the nature of God to treat people as hostages. Yet thousands were swayed, and the goal of the campaign was met. Success does not, however, make something right. This and several other incidences cost the Oral Roberts ministry credibility and money. Ultimately, manipulation and erroneous theology will damage the church and its ministry. Current struggles within Oral Roberts' ministry confirm this. Preachers must be careful not to misinform their markets.

There are innumerable levels on which a preacher can misinform a congregation about giving. One of the most frequently used yet faulty appeals is that "we give in order to receive blessings from God." As is the case with most heresies, there is a hint of truth in this statement.

I have known a lot of generous people who felt blessed by God. Not one has said to me, "I wish I had not been generous." However, the motivation for Christian giving does not rest in our expectation of receiving a material blessing from God. That theology paints a picture of God as a giant vending machine. The more one gives — the more money or faithfulness one puts in — the more material blessings God bestows. The focus on material dividends creates a heresy.

Such a theology does not stand up under close biblical scrutiny. John the Baptist gave of himself until his head was served on a platter. Jesus gave of himself until he hung on a cross. Paul gave of himself and was threatened, jailed, and beaten. Tradition has it that the Apostle Peter gave of himself until he was crucified upside-down by Emperor Nero in Rome. Faithfulness, financial or otherwise, does not bring an easy life. We cannot buy God's blessings. The Christian gives out of a thankful heart for God's blessings, even when physical or economic life is difficult.

An old legend relates how, after his conversion, Zacchaeus would get up very early every morning and leave the house. His wife, curious to know what he was doing, followed him one morning. Stopping at a well, Zacchaeus lowered a bucket and filled it with water. He took the water to a sycamore tree. After cleaning the rubbish from around the tree, Zacchaeus emptied the water at the tree's base. He then climbed into the tree's branches and appeared to be in deep contemplation. Zacchaeus' wife emerged from her hiding place and asked what he was doing. Zacchaeus replied, "This is the tree where I found Christ!"

What is the Christian motivation for giving? It is thanksgiving! God has given us all that we have. God has given his Son, Jesus. What more can God give? We do not give in order to receive. We are already recipients of God's gracious goodness. We give in order to say "Thank you!"

Zacchaeus' loving action was not performed to receive anything. He already had everything! His act of caring for the tree was one of response.

Therein lies the nature of genuine stewardship. God has blessed us, wherever we are and whoever we are. All that we have is a gift. God even gives us responsibility in this world. We have become co-creators with God. God has been faithful to the covenant. Our faithful living and giving are a response to God's love. Since all that we have is a gift, then every part of life is touched by the elemental nature of stewardship.

Why is preaching for giving important? It is important not just from a financial viewpoint. That limits the issue far too much. Preaching for giving touches the totality of life. When the preacher proclaims healthy stewardship sermons without manipulation or erroneous theology, the hearer is invited simply to respond to God's goodness. It is a matter of conversion. Nothing is more basic in the gospel.

SILENCE IN THE PULPIT

The final pitfall that we mention here is the danger of being silent. How tempting it is to say little or nothing about giving. If the church struggles or fails in its financial responsibilities, then the preacher can exonerate herself or himself by being "above the fray." One preacher told me that church finances were the sole responsibility of the laity. If the church did not succeed in its finances, it was not his fault; it was the fault of the laity. This line of thought pits the preacher against the laity and is a recipe for failure. The preacher must accept the mantle of leadership. That leadership should not be autocratic, authoritarian, or manipulative. Good leaders share responsibilities, challenge people, and provide opportunities for others to lead. Good leaders, pastors, and preachers do not excuse themselves and dodge their responsibility. Silence from the pulpit is reflective of poor leadership!

One of my preacher friends discovered that the key for her stewardship preaching was wrapped up in simply helping God to celebrate. In one particularly powerful sermon, she tells of ways we can help God to celebrate. One man in her church cleans out the pencil holders on the backs of the pews. God celebrates because this servant is not willing to settle for anything less than the best he can give.

God also celebrates when we learn that there is joy in giving. In another sermon this same preacher told the story of an elementary school teacher whose class gave her a party to show their appreciation. The children brought gifts and refreshments. One student, John, did not bring anything because his mother would not allow him. "We are poor," she said. "We cannot afford anything." But when John got to school he made a card. He wrote, "I love you, Mrs. Griner." He put X's and O's and flowers around the edge. Taped to the card was a dime and seven pennies. The teacher wanted to return the money but could not when she saw the joy that John experienced in giving. God is like that.

In yet another story, my friend helped her congregation see that God celebrates when, out of our abundance, we give our best. She told the sad story of a church that put an ad in the newspaper: "Leave your wallet at home. Plenty of churches just want your money. Come worship with us." In her sermon she reflected on the fact that she does not want to be part of a church like that. She wants to give. Giving brings joy because, in sharing to make a difference for others, we participate in that for which we are created.[2] Her sermon rang throughout with a note of celebration.

Silence from the pulpit was not an option for my preacher friend. It is not an option for any of us! With joy we proclaim that it matters what we give, because our giving is deeply and permanently connected to our spirituality.

To Summarize

The high road of preaching for giving is surrounded by pitfalls. I am convinced that most people want to give (after all, we are made for this), but we can easily be thrown off track. The task of the preacher is to articulate the connection among spirituality, faith, and financial stewardship without becoming entrapped in one or more of the pitfalls.

Individual preachers will often find that they have tendencies to misstep in the direction of specific pitfalls. Either by temperament or by training, one will tend to ignore the market while another attacks it; one will tend to misinform the market while another is tempted to silence. If we can recognize the pitfalls, however, then we can also claim the freeing and healing power of Christ. Or, to use a more dramatic image, we can "name our own demons." By the power of the Spirit, this naming of the demons will enable us to move toward a more holistic praxis of preaching for giving.

6 | LAYING THE GROUNDWORK

Preaching is not a simple task. Homiletics professors struggle with finding methods that will aid their students in sermon preparation and delivery. I recall a story, perhaps apocryphal, about the late G. Ray Jordan, an outstanding homiletics instructor at Candler School of Theology, Emory University. Jordan arranged for his students to preach in front of the class as part of their training. One of the students in Jordan's class was serving as a student local pastor while attending seminary. On his designated day, this student preached a sermon to the homiletics class. At the close of the sermon, Dr. Jordan proceeded to identify all of the weaknesses in the young preacher's presentation. The student defended himself by recalling that when he had preached the same sermon to his congregation, five people had cried. Dr. Jordan's memorable reply was, "Son, after hearing that sermon, I can understand why they cried."

I am not a homiletics professor. My call and joy in life is to serve as the pastor of a local church. Most of you who are reading this book are in the same kind of setting. In spite of the similar settings, there are differences among us as individual preachers. Thank God for the differences that exist. We are not clones of each other. While the differences preclude the possibility of any simplistic formula for preaching financial stewardship sermons, there are some "rules of thumb" that are pertinent to all of us as we prepare to preach. This chapter will outline some of the basic elements of preparing sermons and preaching for giving.

PRACTICE WHAT YOU PREACH

An old wisdom saying begins, "What's good for the goose . . . ." It is imperative that we take a look at ourselves before we begin preparing financial stewardship sermons. If we are serious about proclaiming scriptural holiness in regard to financial stewardship, then we must not be hypocritical in our own giving. Asking our markets, our congregations, to do something that we are unwilling to do is inexcusable. Preachers who call others to commitment must be committed themseves. Those who seek to circumvent this basic rule of leadership will ultimately fail. Their preaching will lack authenticity.

During the catastrophic famine in Somalia in 1992 my family decided to make a special "second-mile" gift to fight world hunger. My wife, Susan, and I talked about it with our children. It was important to us that they see the pain and recognize the need. As a family, we discussed the amount we should give. I wrote a check and gave it to Susan so that she could place it in the offering plate the next Sunday. However, God was not yet through with the discussion. Emily, our younger child, came back to the kitchen and placed every penny, nickel, dime, quarter, and dollar she had in front of me and said, "Daddy, I want to give it all to those hungry kids." Her unlimited generosity put my limited generosity to shame.

That event (as well as others) caused me to reflect on my motivation for giving. As a preacher, how do I feel about giving? This question is key. If I, as a preacher, feel ambivalent about my own giving, how can I call others to give? My preaching will lack integrity and my sermons will not preach. The congregation will sense the lack of integrity.

I believe in tithing. While tithing is not a ticket to heaven, it is a disciplined way of participating in the kingdom of God. There have been times when Susan and I have had to think through our family budget in order to tithe our income. This has brought nothing but healthy consequences. In keeping with its origins in the worship practices of Israel, tithing reminds us of what is important in life! We love to give, and over the last few years have moved beyond the tithe in our giving patterns. I do not share this information with a sense of self-righteous braggadocio. (There will always be room for growth in my giving! That is the nature of Christian giving.) My proclamation of the Word related to financial stewardship, however, is directly related to my own giving.

When I stand in front of my congregation and preach for giving, I share firsthand the joy of giving. When I give of my money to the church, I know that the money given is a reflection of my work and energy. My money is a way of changing intangible faith into tangible faith.

As a preacher and leader, I have no difficulties with my congregation knowing what I give. When I tell them that I give more than a tithe of my gross salary, they can figure out the specifics of exactly how much that is, for they are the ones who set my salary. Tone is very important in sharing this information. It must be done joyfully, not judgmentally. There should be a trust level established with the congregation prior to challenging them in this way. In observing congregations where the pastor lovingly lets the congregation know her or his level of commitment, I have seen a positive shift in giving.

What kind of subtle messages does the preacher give in revealing a personal level of commitment? The preacher is indicating a strong love of God. It also becomes apparent that this preacher loves and is committed to the local church. Finally, I believe that our congregations see this as an act of love for them. Modeling good stewardship for the laity is important if our sermons are to be effective.

Giving is not a drudgery! Giving is a joyful opportunity! Through our giving, God is able to make an impact in this world. Does your congregation see joy and commitment in your giving?

DO YOUR HOMEWORK!

There can be no excuse for lack of spiritual or intellectual preparation in sermon construction. The minutes the preacher spends in the pulpit proclaiming the Word are critical. It is imperative that the good news be joyfully proclaimed. Yet some of us undermine the very words we speak from the pulpit through lack of preparation. We do not read, write, or think. Our lack of preparation is embarrassingly evident in our preaching. Particularly when preaching for giving, we have a tendency to underprepare. Since we have not yet discovered the wonderful joy of proclaiming an invitation to be faithful givers, we simply use the same formula we used last year. In blind and naive optimism, we think, "Well, it didn't work last year, but maybe it will work this year." We become angry when, once again, the response of the congregation is less than positive and affirming. The words we say from the pulpit are important. These words merit some significant time and consideration prior to entering the pulpit.

Jesus understood the importance of words. Interestingly enough, he defines the unforgivable sin as a sin of speech rather than a sin of action: ". . . by your words you will be justified, and by your words you will be condemned" (Matthew 12:37). What we say matters! Preaching is important enough to spend time in preparation!

One of the deadliest diseases for preachers is cynicism. Perhaps because we spend so much time using words, we can come to a point of believing that nothing we say really matters. Our sermons begin to sound alike. This happens because we are depressed and are not doing our homework. Every preacher goes through "dry spells," but it is imperative to stay faithful to the task. Peter Bohler, the Moravian preacher, gave this advice to a cynical and shaky John Wesley: ". . . preach faith till you have it and then because you have it, you will preach faith."[1] That is still good advice.

Why should our preaching be subject to tempestuous feelings and emotions? Our lives must be based on faithfulness rather than on emotional ups and downs. It is a joy to preach when everything is great. What happens when life is less than perfect?

One of the first things to include in our "homework" is prayer. In an age of instantaneous gratification, prayer is almost an anomaly. Prayer gives an opportunity to tap into the source of our power and strength. God listens and speaks to us in our prayer life. Prayer is a dialogue rather than a monologue. Preparing to preach must be bathed in an attitude of prayer. Ironically, the tempo and pressures of ministry today can crowd out the quiet time of worship, prayer, and meditation. To allow this to happen, however, is to court disaster. It is to cut the umbilical cord that connects us to God. The farther a plane flies, the more fuel it needs and the more ground service it requires. The longer an orchestra plays, the more the instruments must be retuned. Preachers are busy people. The more intense the pressure and schedule, the more imperative it is that we guard disciplined times for prayer, meditation, and worship.

Another important piece of homework is to plan sermons as part of a total worship experience. Preaching occurs within the context of the total service of worship. Poorly planned worship can have an adverse impact on a fine sermon. Is your worship exciting and invitational in nature? Does your congregation look forward to worship? If not, what homework can you do to transform worship into an experience where God's Spirit can be at work?

Will Willimon writes about changing our understanding of the very nature of worship. Some of us have made the pulpit an egocentric pedestal. We, along with the choir and other worship leaders, perform the worship for the audience or congregation. Willimon contends that this is an erroneous theology of worship. Worship is the work of all the people: preacher, choir, worship leaders, soloists, and congregation. The only audience is God.[2] Worship is not a show! It is a corporate and shared response to God's goodness. Worship can and should be planned to make everyone present feel that they are part of the activity of worship. One does not watch worship. One participates in worship. What kind of feeling is generated by your service of worship? Do your people worship with you?

Please do not expect your preaching for giving to happen easily. There is homework involved. I predict that you will find a direct correlation between the work you do (studying, praying, planning worship) and the success of the sermons you preach on financial stewardship. Preachers must do their homework!

LISTEN TO THE LAITY

The laity must help in the development of an overall plan for financial stewardship in a local church. Many laypersons have expertise in areas related to financial stewardship. Tapping their gifts will only bring strength to the process.

Several years ago a committee in my local church decided that they wanted to do something significant for a soup kitchen ministry in our city. They prayed and brainstormed about this problem for several weeks. In doing the research, they discovered that it took $.37 to feed a hungry person one meal. The committee founded "The $.37 Club." Two payments per year will take care of the meals for one (or more) indigent persons for that year. Tens of thousands of dollars are generated each year in my local church for the soup kitchen. People want to be members of "The $.37 Club." The impact of this ministry eventually grew beyond our local church. The club has spread throughout the city and now provides a large percentage of total receipts for the soup kitchen ministry. This is just a sample of what laity can do when they are released to be creative.

As the laity dream and plan, they begin to feel a sense of ownership in the plans. Financial plans made from an autocratic or authoritarian stance fail because the laity are not a part of the decision-making process. For example, how many people are involved in the budget setting and planning at your church? A good rule of thumb is that at least 15 percent of your congregation should be involved. (If possible, include even more than this.) Through committees, boards, sessions, and meetings the laity need to talk about perceived needs. When the budget is finally adopted, the laypeople in a local church need to be able to point to this document and say, "I had a part in building the budget." Ownership brings interest. Interest breeds responsibility. Responsibility creates higher levels of giving.

When preaching for giving, draw from the dreams and discussions that have taken place with the laity in your local church. Let them motivate your preparation for preaching. Share specific examples of the local church process. One pastor told the congregation that she thought the dreams and excitement of the laity had caused the budget to be set too high, but then she realized she was limiting God's Spirit. That congregation is healthy and doing well because the laity pushed the pastor to dream bigger dreams.

SELECT LAY LEADERSHIP CAREFULLY

One of my retired preacher friends told me to always be careful not to build my foundation with "loose bricks." He was referring to how careful preachers must be in selecting and cultivating lay leadership in the local church. In some of our congregations, the key lay leaders are tragically uncommitted in their own giving patterns. This lack of commitment on their part undermines the entire process of growth in the area of financial stewardship. How can someone who is basically uncommitted to generous giving challenge someone else to give generously? It cannot be done. An active alcoholic cannot lead another alcoholic to sobriety. A sober alcoholic can help another alcoholic change her or his life. So it is with giving. Laity who occupy key positions must be committed to giving of their financial resources so that they can help others grow.

In this light, I want to raise an important question: "Should a pastor have access to giving records in the local church?" I believe that this kind of access is imperative. How can true leadership be selected apart from this consideration? If giving is reflective of one's spirituality, then the preacher should know this vital information. Jesus watched as people made their offerings. Some made large offerings, but he became excited when he saw the widow put in two mites. If our giving reflects of what is happening inside us, then what we give is important. In keeping with Jesus' example, however, the amount is not as important as the level (or percentage) of giving. Some of my key lay leaders give modest amounts, but I know that they are truly sacrificing because of unemployment or a bad year in business. Others in my church who give large amounts have not begun to discover the joy of giving sacrificially.

My financial secretary is aware that I want to know when anyone's giving pattern shifts up or down significantly. Often, this shift is a barometer of what is taking place in an individual or family. Giving patterns are a way of taking the spiritual pulse of a congregation. Good pastoral leadership will address issues of change and seek to minister to those in need of pastoral care.

The pastor must never abuse such privileged information. Abuse of this information should be challenged immediately. However, most of the preachers I know are trustworthy and know how to handle such information discreetly. They can use the knowledge to propel the church toward more effective mission and ministry.

PUT FEET ON YOUR SERMONS

Preaching right-brain, invitational sermons related to financial stewardship takes intentionality. Everything we have said thus far supports this truth. It is also important, however, to deal with the pragmatic aspect of how the congregation responds to the call for commitment. In short, we must consider how to put feet on our sermons.

There are quite a few financial commitment campaigns available that will help the preacher provide an opportunity for the congregation to respond. What should one look for in a good, holistic, healthy campaign? *First*, a good financial campaign will involve large numbers of laity. There will be several committees functioning during the campaign. These committees should involve approximately 25 percent of the congregation. Organization and planning are crucial. The greater number of laity involved in planning and running the campaign, the more likely it is that the campaign will be successful.

Second, the financial commitment campaign needs to help the congregation make a connection between giving and spirituality. If the campaign fails at this point, then the gospel is thwarted. For this reason I shy away from gimmicks in giving campaigns. This aspect of Christian life is too crucial to be denigrated by gimmicks. Good campaigns should incorporate prayer, worship, and Bible study to encourage and motivate the congregation.

Third, the campaign, while providing structure and organization, needs to be flexible enough for the local church to tell its own story. The campaign needs to be customized rather than generic. Each congregation has good news to share. How is this church involved in mission? What is the focus of ministry in this holy place? How have lives changed? If a church cannot answer these questions with some specificity, then it really is not a church. Answering these questions should bring joy to *every* congregation, regardless of size. A good financial commitment campaign will help a church celebrate the Lord's presence and tell its story of service. This is key because great motivation lies in celebration. Here is an opportunity to "bang the drums" and "blow the trumpets." This celebrating is done for the glory of God!

Fourth, a good giving campaign does not rely on existing church committees for leading the campaign. "New blood" is sometimes needed to provide leadership and motivation. Here is an opportunity to challenge new members as well as old members who have been sitting on the sidelines. The chair of the campaign should be a well-respected person in the church. It is imperative that this individual be a strong giver. Plus, the chair should be *excited* about the campaign. Do not invite a negative person to chair the stewardship campaign. In other positions of leadership in the campaign, people who are peripherally involved in the church (but good givers) can be used. This will aid the church by assimilating and training more people to provide leadership in the church.

Without question, some of the strongest financial commitment campaigns are based on what Don Joiner calls "cycle theory."[3] The Stewardship Office of the General Board of Discipleship of The United Methodist Church suggests using a four-year cycle for giving campaigns. The first campaign would involve an every member visitation. This can be healthy for all churches. The second campaign is built around the concept of group meetings to provide information and motivation. The third-year campaign would focus on a Commitment Sunday. The last year would be one of the circulation packet programs. I admit that some circulation packet programs are based entirely on gimmicks. However, there are some that educate and inspire the congregation. Do your research and choose wisely.

Rather than doing the same campaign year after year, using the cycle approach provides variety in the use of skills and insights. This strengthens the life of the whole church. The cycle approach also provides a long-range plan for where the church is headed. When the cycle has ended, the church simply starts over. What a help it is not to have a mighty struggle over what financial commitment campaign should be done each year!

Just Do It!

A couple in my church gave me a T-shirt with that famous advertising slogan printed on the front. I like that shirt! The slogan is a call to action.

The groundwork for effective stewardship preaching is really a network of actions. Exciting worship and a good stewardship campaign strengthen the environment for good preaching. At the same time, in large measure, they depend on it. Likewise, strong pastoral leadership is needed for training and motivating laity; but working with laity "in the trenches" to create a total congregational strategy can only enhance the pastor's ability to lead in gracious, collegial, and invitational ways. Preaching for giving does not really leave any room for a "hands off" approach. Unapologetic, benevolent leadership from the pastor is a must. Laity in our churches desire gracious leadership. Just do it!

7 | HOLY BOLDNESS

Stewardship preaching in the U.S. today is at a crossroads. Stewardship is central to the spiritual health of the church, and preaching is crucial to stewardship. Yet many preachers have responded to the current situation by becoming timid in leadership and proclamation. As a result, our congregations often display uncertainty about their own financial stewardship. Nothing could improve the situation more than a new manifestation of holy boldness in the way we preach for giving.

To be sure, in our history, culture, and experience there are reasons why we may doubt this call to holy boldness. We have seen a kind of "boldness" — in the excesses of revivalistic manipulation — that is not *holy*. We have witnessed a kind of "holiness" — accustomed to the privatization of wealth in capitalist economy — that is not *bold*. In the face of such counterfeits, what are the alternatives? Must we choose silence in order to avoid the appearance of pandering? Shall we accept marginalization in order to avoid the charge of meddling? Such reasonings and alternatives serve neither the preacher, the church, nor the gospel well.

One thing is clear: Scripture approaches the subject of money and material possessions with its own kind of holy boldness. Old Testament stories make clear the connection between giving and faith in God's faithfulness. Likewise, Jesus made clear that our capacity for giving is nothing short of a matter of salvation. One cannot become a Christian apart from responding to God's grace. Ingratitude and lack of generosity are not options for Christians, because they would imply that we have yet to understand or respond to the grace and love offered by God. From a biblical point of view, the bottom line is this: How do we say "thank you" to God?

The kind of holy boldness that we need today, however, is not so much a matter of shouting louder, or causing a big sensation. (That, after all, might only lead us to those whose goal is mere market manipulation.) Rather, our holy boldness must be one that uncovers the depth and breadth of stewardship in all of life, in season and out of season. We can find this kind of holy boldness if we are willing to be creative and challenge the "rules" that often govern expectations about when, where, how, and why to preach for giving.

WHEN TO PREACH FOR GIVING

For most of us, there is probably a time of the year when we focus on financial stewardship. Preaching for giving is important during this designated time of the year. However, financial stewardship should not be just a seasonal emphasis. While one might prepare several sermons focused on financial stewardship during the campaign, preaching for giving is a year-round proposition. Parts of many sermons throughout the year should mention financial stewardship. Can you think of any part of the biblical narrative that has nothing to do with financial stewardship? I cannot.

The lectionary provides preachers with an opportunity to follow the primary biblical themes as they unfold. Advent focuses on the first and second comings of Christ. What are the implications of Advent? How are we to prepare for Christ? Giving of ourselves and our resources must be a major part of preparing the way for Christ.

Epiphany focuses on the Light of the World. Like the Magi, we make our way to the manger bringing gifts. Missions usually are emphasized during this season. Preaching for giving should occur naturally in Epiphany.

Lent is, once again, a time of preparation. In honest reflection we recognize our sinfulness. Sin creates the reality of the cross, but in the cross there is forgiveness. If God loves me enough to die for me, how should I respond? What does the cross say about giving? What does the cross imply about sacrifice?

Eastertide is unmatched joy. Death cannot hold Christ! The resurrection prompts us to confront our fears and doubts. The glorious mystery of the resurrection propels us to holy living. Giving is an integral part of holy living.

Pentecost signals the arrival of the incomparable presence of God's Holy Spirit. This Spirit infuses the church with power. How do we respond to the Spirit? What does it mean for the church to be in ministry? Has God's Holy Spirit changed our lives?

As you can see, there is not a single part of the Bible or the church year that is devoid of financial reflection. God's love invites a response from us. Our preaching needs to be reflective of this balance: God gives, God invites; we respond, we serve.

Please do not misunderstand me. I am not advocating that you "beat your congregation over the head" with money sermons. That would be counterproductive. However, it is also catastrophic to assign stewardship to a season. This creates negative feelings: "Oh no, it's financial campaign time. I don't need to hear this. Maybe I'll just stay home." Congregations need to hear preaching for giving frequently so that stewardship is viewed as a normal part of Christian living. This year-round awareness will make the financial stewardship campaign stronger, for the campaign will be viewed as a normal, natural part of church life rather than "the church's pitch for your money."

In a series of sermons I preached on the Lord's Prayer, I reflected on the implications of praying, ". . . Thy kingdom come, Thy will be done on earth, as it is in heaven." The door was wide open for me to say that God's kingdom is directly related to doing God's will. Anyone who says that they have met Jesus and has not dealt with what it means to do God's will with one's finances has not truly dealt with Jesus. Jesus challenges and invites us to consider specifically our role in bringing God's kingdom on earth by doing God's will in our lives. This reflection was just a small part of the sermon. It was a natural thing to say, even though it was not financial stewardship time.

Preach sensitively for giving throughout the church year. In doing this, you will be exhibiting healthy and holistic stewardship. Your financial campaign will then take place within the larger context of the connection between spirituality and giving.

WHERE TO PREACH FOR GIVING

Part of our creativity should be channeled into thinking through where we are to preach for giving. The most obvious response is, of course, in our own pulpits. We can proclaim the Word to our people better than anyone from the outside.

But there are other places where we need to be "preaching." First, there are individuals in your congregation who need a pointed, specific visit from their pastor to discuss giving. Yes, I know that this can present difficulties. However, I also want you to recognize the joys that can come in this individual process of proclamation and preaching. I once asked a man for $100,000 for a building program. He was a wealthy corporate executive who had just lost his job. In no way was he offended by my request. To the contrary, he indicated that he was honored that I would trust him enough to ask. He pledged $50,000 to the program.

While you do not want to be constantly "begging," it is important to know and trust some key laypersons who welcome the opportunity to talk with you about the needs of the church and their giving. In such conversations, I encourage you to be specific in your requests. Your openness from the pulpit regarding financial stewardship will set the stage for some private, confidential visits with particular individuals. While you may not receive exactly what you request, generally I have found that laypersons feel honored to be approached and challenged by their preacher in this direct and personal way. My feedback in "preaching" to individuals has been positive.

Second, use your Christian education program to undergird and strengthen your preaching for giving. Perhaps you need to "teach" stewardship to an adult Sunday school class. One's teaching ministry can open new doors of understanding for one's preaching ministry.

Third, use the prayer groups in your church to help in your preparation for preaching for giving. Be open about your concerns. Make the concerns a matter of prayer. Remember, a primary task for the preacher is to help laypersons make a connection among financial resources, giving, faithfulness, and spirituality. Prayer groups could be a good place to start a financial campaign. If the members of the group are able to see the connection among prayer, giving, and spirituality, they will become advocates for your preaching!

HOW TO PREACH FOR GIVING

The question about how to preach is more than a matter of technical expertise. Above all, it is a matter of attitude, affection, and character. If we really believe the good news about the new way of life made available in Christ, then how will this affect the character of our presence in the pulpit?

Be confident! We are not proclaiming a secondhand aspect of the gospel. God's word says much about giving. If we preach the scripture, we will proclaim the joy and challenge of giving.

Be specific! The most successful financial campaigns and financial stewardship sermons are able to give the congregation reasons to give. Avoid the trap of building the campaign and your sermons around the general budget of the church. Look at the budget closely. What within the budget reflects mission and ministry? Where in the budget is the church involved in service? Tell these stories in an exciting, right-brain manner.

One of the exciting ways my local church tells the story is through a ministries fair. Each group or ministry in the church is invited to set up a booth that reflects its ministry and identity. What a joyous occasion to see people looking at these exhibits and even signing up for different areas of service. This climate can be an extension of your preaching for giving. Leading the congregation in such projects promotes community and gives the church reasons to celebrate.

Avoid crisis appeals. Some churches I know appear to be in a constant state of crisis. The issue of financial stewardship is never raised unless there is a problem. The perception of the laity, then, is that stewardship is a negative issue. Giving is a part of our daily walk with God. Avoid the temptation of consigning all discussion of financial stewardship to crisis-driven events.

Why Preach for Giving?

If one theme resonates through this book, it is that people become interested in giving for one primary reason: Because they (we) are made that way. According to scripture, we discover the very essence and joy of life in the Spirit of the God who gives us all things. Relational theology demands a response. Those who have received grace are compelled, out of the reception of grace, to consider their own giving. Therefore, giving is a biblical imperative, and stewardship is a lens through which Christians view the world.

In traditional language, giving is a response to conversion and justification. If "God so loved the world that he gave . . ." (John 3:16), then how are we to respond? Our people want to hear the good news, and having heard it they want to say "thank you" to God. Giving is a mirror, a reflection of one's understanding of and relationship with God. The person who meets Christ looks for ways to serve and give.

Early in my ministry I started a financial stewardship sermon with a half-apology. After the sermon, several of the laypersons reproved me for the apology. They could not understand my timidity in preaching for giving. They were right! Preaching for giving should not be done apologetically. Why do we preach for giving? We do so because God has given to us and called us into the joy of giving to others.

A Concluding Word to Preachers

On occasion I have been privileged to preach revivals in churches. Not only do I enjoy visiting other congregations, but I have found that spending time with the host pastors always enriches my ministry. These experiences, however, have convinced me of the fact that great preaching should not be judged on a limited number of sermons. Revival preaching, with its relatively short time period, may be exciting, but it does not approach the depth a local pastor can reach by preaching every week. Preaching can only be great when done over an extended period of time with a congregation.

There is a wide difference between a great preacher and a preacher of great sermons. A great preacher is wrapped up in the totality of communal life with the congregation. Great preachers develop strong relationships. Their proclamation grows from these relationships. They are fed by their people and, in turn, they feed their people. The relationship is reciprocal.

On the other hand, preachers of great sermons are primarily technicians. They may craft their sermons with skill, but their lack of involvement in the congregation creates a setting that limits God's Word. Jesus told an allegorical parable that illustrates this issue. Great preachers preach to commonly fertile soil due to the fact that they have cared for and "worked" the soil. Because of the relationship and trust level that have developed over a period of time, the congregation "hears" the proclaimed Word with anticipation and expectation. Preachers of great sermons may excite everyone for a brief period of time, but their sermons, because of lack of relationship, have no roots. They have not "worked" the soil. The seed may sprout quickly, but there is no depth to the soil (Matthew 13:3-9).

Great preaching, then, is determined over an extended period of time with our congregations. Preaching for giving is at its strongest in this setting. While every preacher may not have the same potential of being a preacher of great *sermons*, every preacher can be a great *preacher*. I would much rather be known by my congregation as a great preacher than as a preacher of great sermons. In whatever setting you find yourself, God has given you the ability to be a great preacher. Great preachers know and love their people. Great preachers work hard on sermon preparation. Great preachers trust God to use even imperfect, blemished efforts for his glory.

God's Holy Spirit uses preachers in proclaiming the joy of giving. Any preacher's hesitancy in preaching for giving can be transformed by God into a courageous, invitational, and loving proclamation for financial stewardship. God will be with you as you prepare. God's Spirit will lead you as you study. Preach for giving with holy boldness!

ENDNOTES

Chapter 1

[1]Henri Nouwen, *The Wounded Healer* (Garden City, New York: Image Books, 1972), pp. 81-83.

[2]Fred Craddock, *Preaching* (Nashville: Abingdon Press, 1985), pp. 177 ff.

[3]Donald F. Chatfield, *Dinner with Jesus* (Grand Rapids: Zondervan, 1988), p. 9.

[4]Henri Nouwen, pp. 81-94.

[5]Russell A. Lockhart, "Coins and Psychological Change," in *Soul and Money* (Dallas: Spring Publications, 1982), p. 14.

[6]W. D. Goodger, ed., "Always Talking About Money," in *Spotlighting Stewardship* (Don Mills, Ontario: The United Church of Canada, 1981), p. 66.

[7]Haddon Robinson, "Preaching on Money: When You've Gone to Meddlin'," *Preaching*, Vol. VI, No. 5 (March-April, 1991), p. 2.

[8]Stephen Hart and David Krueger, "Integrating Faith and Work," *The Christian Century*, Vol. 109, No. 22 (July 15, 1992), p. 683.

Chapter 2

[1]Williston Walker, *A History of the Christian Church*, Third Edition (New York: Charles Scribner's Sons, 1970), p. 305.

[2]Ibid., p. 307.

[3]Ibid., p. 308.

[4]John Wesley, *The Works of John Wesley*, Vol. II, Sermons 2 (Nashville: Abingdon, 1984), pp. 263-80.

[5]Wellman, J. Werner, *The Wesleyan Movement in the Industrial Revolution* (London: Longmans, 1930), p. 33.

[6]John Wesley, *Wesley's Works*, Vol. VI (New York: Carleton and Porter, 1856), pp. 176-77.

[7]Francis J. McConnell, *John Wesley* (New York: Abingdon, 1939), pp. 262-63. Copyright renewal 1967 by Eva H. McConnell. Used by permission of the publisher, Abingdon Press.

[8]Wesley, *Works*, Vol. II, p. 264.

[9]Charles Edward White, "Four Lessons on Money," *Christian History*, Vol. VII, No. 3 (Issue 19), p. 24.

[10]Ibid.

[11]Ibid., p. 21.

[12]McConnell, *Wesley*, pp. 263, 271.

[13]Wesley, *Works*, Vol II, p. 284.

[14]Ibid., pp. 284-86.

[15]John Wesley, *Wesley's Works*, Vol. VII (Peabody, Mass.: Hendrickson Publishers, Inc., 1984), p. 360.

[16]Leland Ryken, "That Which God Hath Lent Thee," *Christian History*, Vol. VII, No. 3 (Issue 19), p. 12.

[17]Virgil Hartgerink, "The Protestant Ethic Prosperity," *Christian History*, Vol. VI, No. 2, p. 21.

[18]Ibid.

[19]Leland Ryken, "That Which God Hath Lent Thee," p. 15.

[20]G.A.E. Salstrand, *The Story of Stewardship* (Grand Rapids: Baker Books, 1956), p. 13.

[21]Ibid., p. 14.

[22]Ibid., p. 19.

[23]Sydney Ahlstrom, *A Religious History of the American People*, Vol. 1 (Garden City, New York: Image Books, 1975), p. 530.

[24]Benjamin Franklin, *Autobiography* (New York: Washington Press, 1940), pp. 130-31.

25Ahlstrom, *American People*, p. 350.

26Ibid., p. 351.

27Yngve Brilioth, *A Brief History of Preaching* (Philadelphia: Fortress Press, 1965), p. 173.

28Salstrand, *Stewardship*, p. 26.

29Ibid., p. 27.

30Ibid., p. 31.

31Ibid.

32Ibid., p. 33.

33Robert Bellah et al., *Habits of the Heart: Individualism and Commitment in American Life* (New York: Harper and Row, 1985).

34This admonition was given in an address to a Vision 2000 rally for the South Georgia Annual Conference of The United Methodist Church meeting in Macon, Georgia, on January 16, 1993.

Chapter 3

1Bishop Carder presented this outline for theology in his address to delegates of the Southeastern Jurisdictional Conference in the summer of 1992.

2David L. Heetland, *Fundamentals of Fundraising* (Nashville: Discipleship Resources, 1989), pp. 13-14.

3Markus Barth, *The Anchor Bible*, Vol. 34 (Doubleday and Co., 1974), pp. 97-98.

4Ibid.

5Isaac Watts, "When I Survey the Wondrous Cross," *The United Methodist Hymnal* (Nashville: The United Methodist Publishing House, 1989), No. 299.

6Daniel Kauffman, *Managers with God: Continuing the Work Christ Began* (Scottdale, Pennsylvania: Herald Press, 1990), p. 32.

7Rhodes Thompson, *Stewards Shaped by Grace* (St. Louis: CBP Press, 1990), p. vii.

Chapter 4

[1]James B. Ashbrook, *Faith and Ministry in Light of the Double Brain* (Bristol, Indiana: Wyndham Hall Press, 1989), p. 7.

[2]Ibid., p. 8.

[3]W. D. Goodger, ed., "Always Talking About Money," in *Spotlighting Stewardship* (Don Mills, Ontario: The United Church of Canada, 1981), p. 66.

[4]John A. Sanford, *The Kingdom Within* (San Francisco: Harper and Row, 1987), p. 29.

Chapter 5

[1]Benjamin Franklin, *Autobiography* (New York: Washington Square Press, 1940), pp. 120-21.

[2]This sermon was preached by the Rev. Leigh Ann Raynor at Cross Keys United Methodist Church, Macon, Georgia.

Chapter 6

[1]John Wesley, *Journal*, Vol. I, Standard Ed., Nehemiah Curnock, ed. (1909-16), p. 422.

[2]William Willimon, *The Gospel for the Person Who Has Everything* (Valley Forge, Pennsylvania: Judson Press, 1978), p. 64.

[3]Don Joiner, "Celebrate Stewardship," a publication of the Stewardship Unit of the General Board of Discipleship, The United Methodist Church, Volume 4, Number 4 (Dec. 1991).